D0907328

PLATO
REPUBLIC I

PLATO
REPUBLIC I

Edited with Introduction,
Notes and Vocabulary by
D.J. ALLAN

Bristol Classical Press

This impression 2002

This edition published 1993 by
Bristol Classical Press
an imprint of
Gerald Duckworth & Co. Ltd.
61 Frith Street, London W1D 3JL
Tel: 020 7434 4242
Fax: 020 7434 4420
inquiries@duckworth-publishers.co.uk
www.ducknet.co.uk

First published in 1940 by Methuen & Co. Ltd.
Second edition, revised, 1944
Reprinted with a new Preface, 1953

© 1940, 1944 by D.J. Allan

All rights reserved. No part of this publication
may be reproduced, stored in a retrieval system, or
transmitted, in any form or by any means, electronic,
mechanical, photocopying, recording or otherwise,
without the prior permission of the publisher.

A catalogue record for this book is available
from the British Library

ISBN 1 85399 254 2

Printed in Great Britain by
Antony Rowe Ltd, Eastbourne

PREFACE

I gratefully acknowledge the help which I have received from earlier editions of the *Republic*. Two particularly deserve to be named—the commentary of Adam, which should constantly be consulted to amplify what I have said, and Tucker's edition of the first two books (*The Proem to the Ideal Commonwealth of Plato*). Tucker's standards of logical and grammatical correctness are rather exacting, and Plato does not always live up to them; the edition, however, remains a sound and informative one.

Since I had little alteration to bring to the established text, there seemed to be no need for critical notes or for a discussion of manuscripts, and I have only mentioned divergences of reading where they affect the argument. My text is, except in regard to punctuation, based on that of Burnet.

The question must be raised whether it is a fair proceeding to study this first book in detachment from the dialogue of which it forms merely the first episode. Many scholars have suggested, and some have stated as a confirmed fact, that Book I was composed much earlier than the main part of the *Republic*. Only at a later stage, when he was prepared to give an elaborate answer to those questions about the meaning and value of justice which are here discussed without positive result, did Plato convert the book into the preface to a larger dialogue.

There is no ancient evidence to this effect, nor, indeed, is there any regarding the date of composition of the *Republic* as a whole. But it is held, firstly, that the style and vocabulary of the book are plainly different from those of the remaining nine books of the *Republic*, and, secondly, that the book, taken by itself, is complete and satisfactory, in an artistic if not in a philosophical sense. It leaves the reader without positive ideas; but so do other early dialogues like the *Euthyphro* and *Ion*. These two points must be briefly considered.

(1) The statistical survey of style and vocabulary has proved to be the most effective means of deciding the order of composition of Plato's dialogues. The methods used cannot be explained in detail here, but I venture to suggest that H. von Arnim, in the study which he published in 1912,[1] brought to light some serious weaknesses in the use of statistical methods by all his predecessors save the originator of this style of research, Professor Lewis Campbell. For his own part, Von Arnim isolates for study a single phenomenon, namely, the way in which the minor characters reply to the observations of the chief speaker. He enumerates some recurrent expressions, such as πῶς γαρ οὐκ and πάνυ μὲν οὖν, counts the instances of each in every dialogue, and then by an elaborate calculation determines the affinity between every dialogue and every other, taking separately the books of which longer works, like the *Republic*, are composed. He considers this a suitable subject for a survey which ought to be wholly formal, and independent of preconceived views about the substance of Plato's teaching.

This differs considerably from the use made of style statistics by Campbell in his editions of the *Sophist* and *Politicus* and in Vol. II of Jowett and Campbell's *Republic*. Campbell was concerned with a small group of dialogues which stand apart from the rest of Plato's writings by the use of an artificial and poetical style, and he was easily able, with the assistance of the known fact that the *Laws* is the work of Plato's old age, to prove that these dialogues belong to the later part of his life. Campbell, however, was

[1] *Sprachliche Forschungen zur Chronologie der Platonischen Dialoge.*

careful to make no assertion about a continuous development of Plato's style from the first dialogue to the last.
His successors were more ambitious, and laid themselves
open to the criticisms advanced by Von Arnim.   On the
other hand, it is hard to see how a survey as limited in
scope as his can lead to a pronouncement on so delicate a
problem as the date of the separate books of the *Republic*.
The forms of assent depend, surely, upon the kind of characterization which Plato has chosen to adopt in a particular
passage; and who would presume to say that a writer of
genius could not voluntarily resume his earlier manner for a
special purpose?

(2) The separatists are somewhat vacillating in their
description of Book I—according to them, the piece is
artistically complete, yet it also requires a complement
which Plato was not yet able to provide.   The reader sees
Socrates as a questioner probing conventional beliefs, and
as a critic of false dogmas, but would like to have from him
also at least the outline of a constructive view of the nature
and value of justice.   In other words, having arbitrarily
made Book I separate on the ground that, taken by itself,
it is satisfactory, these critics declare that because it is so
unsatisfactory it must be assigned to an early phase in
Plato's career.

Supposing that we agree to leave aside the question
whether the book is *philosophically* satisfactory, I think that
there are, even in its literary form, features which suggest
that it was written as the prelude to a greater drama, and
that it belongs to the acme of Plato's craftsmanship.

(*a*) Is it true that Book I, disregarding altogether the
absence of positive ideas, is a satisfactory artistic whole?
Is not the presentation of the scene at the beginning far too
long and elaborate in proportion to the debate which fills
the rest of the book?   Why are Plato's brothers Glaucon
and Adeimantus silent throughout the discussion of justice,

with the single exception at 347a, unless because he has an important part in reserve for them? Yes, it may be said, but the book was revised when Plato decided to use it as a preface to the existing *Republic*. But this is to build hypothesis on hypothesis, and it is hard to see how Glaucon and Adeimantus can have been added to the *dramatis personae* without a thorough rehandling, which would almost amount to a rewriting.

(*b*) The narrated form of dialogue seems to have been preferred by Plato not in his earliest writings, but in those later ones in which his dramatic art is most brilliantly displayed, e.g., *Protagoras*, *Phaedo*, *Symposium*, *Republic*, and *Parmenides*. (A study of these dialogues leads to further distinctions—the narrator is sometimes Socrates, sometimes another person; and the narrative is sometimes preceded by a short prefatory dialogue, sometimes not; but this does not affect the present issue.) The narrative gives Plato an opportunity, which a direct dialogue does not afford, for description of the background. He achieves by it the same effect as a dramatist like Shaw does by explicit stage directions. Still later, Plato, evidently becoming less interested in characterization, returned to the direct dialogue, e.g., in the *Cratylus* and *Phaedrus*, the *Theaetetus* trilogy, and all dialogues generally recognized as subsequent to these. Taken with other evidence, this point weighs against the suggestion that Book I can have been an independent early composition. It must be admitted, however, that the *Charmides*, a narrated dialogue which from its content seems plainly to be early, is a clear exception.

To sum up, while this book forms an admirable preface to the *Republic* as a whole, it is not easy to understand what Plato's state of mind would have been if, as is supposed, he wrote the piece independently. None of his admittedly early writings is quite so negative, none shows Socrates so denuded of positive resources. The stylistic evidence

cannot be effectively applied to such a problem as this for
the reasons given; and the other supposed evidence is
internal and is by no means wholly on one side. No ancient
author gives so much as a hint of the independent existence
of Book I. The anecdote that Plato rewrote the first
sentence—see the note on p. 78 below—is too vague to
prove anything. There is, indeed, a story that *two* books
were published separately; but again this, if accepted,
would prove too much. Aulus Gellius, in a discussion of the
rivalry of famous authors, says that Xenophon, being
dissatisfied with Plato's views on government and the ideal
State, as expounded in the first two books of the *Republic*,
wrote in opposition his work on the education of Cyrus.[1]
Gellius does not name his authorities for this statement. A
passage in *Laws* 694 c, in which Plato refers to the education
of Cyrus, does perhaps confirm the fact that he considered
Xenophon's work to be aimed at himself.

However, (*a*) the expression *duo fere libri* cannot represent
the first book alone, and (*b*) a break at the end of the
existing Book II is quite impossible. The reference is
evidently to an ancient arrangement of the *Republic* in six,
instead of ten, books, of which something is known from
other sources. The second book in this arrangement
probably ended at much the same point as the existing
Book III.

This story would have to detain us longer if we were
dealing generally with the possibility that the *Republic* was
published in two parts. But it cannot be said to provide
confirmation of the hypothesis that Book I was composed
earlier and published alone. (See the Introduction by

---

[1] *Noctes Atticae*, XIV 32 'Id etiam esse non sincerae neque amicae
voluntatis indicium crediderunt, quod Xenophon inclyto illi operi
Platonis, quod de optimo statu reipublicae civitatisque administrandae
scriptum est, lectis ex eo duobus fere libris qui primi in vulgus exierant,
opposuit contra conscripsitque diversum regiae administrationis genus,
quod Παιδείας Κύρου inscriptum est.'

A. Diès to the edition of the *Republic* in the Collection Guillaume Budé, published by *Les Belles Lettres*, Paris, 1943: especially pp. xviii—xxii, xxxix—xliii, and cxxiv—cxxxviii.)

The English works which the student will probably find most helpful in considering the argument of this book are these:

R. L. Nettleship, *Lectures on the Republic of Plato*: Macmillan.

H. W. B. Joseph, *Essays in Ancient and Modern Philosophy*: Oxford, Clarendon Press.

G. C. Field, *Plato and his Contemporaries*: Methuen.

F. M. Cornford, *Plato's Republic* (translation with notes): Oxford, Clarendon Press.

Finally, since the appearance of the previous edition of this work, G. B. Kerferd has shown in the *Durham University Journal* (1947) that Plato's account of the views of Thrasymachus is not the burlesque which it has generally been supposed to be. Thrasymachus, though he does not allow his full position to appear at first, presents a consistent view throughout his discussion with Socrates. The confusion which has been attributed to him exists more in the minds of modern scholars and expositors than in that of Plato's Thrasymachus, whose views should not be hastily identified with those expressed by Callicles in the *Gorgias*. Presumably Plato had a faithful recollection of the views of Thrasymachus, as of the other leading sophists. I have not attempted to modify my account of this argument in the light of Mr. Kerferd's interesting views.

D. J. A.

CONTENTS

INTRODUCTION

I

As Plato's own introduction to a larger work, the first
book of the *Republic* is designed on a very simple pattern.
(It is hard to believe the conjecture which has sometimes
been put forward that it was at first an independent
Dialogue written early in Plato's career.)   The question
raised is one which cannot fail to occur to any intelligent
member of a civilized society.   However, this is not the
whole truth.   The elementary fact that ' Justice ' is a
translation of δικαιοσύνη is undeniable : but it does not
follow that the meaning of the Greek and English words
fully coincides.   Again, the special form which Plato
employs to express his opinions—the form of a Dialogue
between historical persons, which has all the appearance
of a real conversation at some definite date—evidently
deserves attention, and must be considered in conjunction
with the meaning of the argument.   For these reasons it
will be best to begin with a short biography of Plato.

He belonged by birth to the privileged classes, for his
father and mother, Ariston and Perictione, were both
representatives of ancient families, which claimed to be
native to Attica. Plato, born in 428-7 B.C., was apparently
the youngest of four children : he had a sister, Potonê,
as well as two brothers, Glaucon and Adeimantus, whom
he depicts with admiration in the *Republic*, and mentions

many times in other Dialogues. Plato's father having died when he was a child, his mother married a relative named Pyrilampês, and had by this second marriage a son named Demos. The explanation of this unusual name is, of course, that the political sympathies of the family were strongly democratic. It had been so, Plato tells us, ever since the time of his ancestor Dropidês, who was an intimate friend of Solon. We are not here concerned with the details of Athenian political history. It is enough to say that the old régime, of which Pericles himself was the most brilliant example, was the government of the masses by their betters under a system of nominal equality. Such a régime was only possible in an era of peace and success. The Peloponnesian war awakened new ambitions for domestic and imperial power in the people, when Pericles was no longer there to keep them in check, and the influence of the old families waned.

Thucydides tells us that the disaster to the Athenian expedition to Sicily had a sobering effect upon the people at home : πάντα τε πρὸς τὸ παραχρῆμα περίδεες, ὅπερ φιλεῖ δῆμος ποιεῖν, ἕτοιμοι ἦσαν εὐτακτεῖν. VIII, I. It was undoubtedly followed by a reaction against democratic institutions. Select ' fraternities ', ἑταίρειαι, bound together by the idea of a return to the form of government which had prevailed before Solon, began to acquire power, and in 411 the Assembly was reorganized and its composition limited to five thousand persons who were rich enough to equip themselves with arms ; and a smaller body of four hundred was appointed to select the five thousand. The interest with which Plato followed these changes may be imagined. He was sixteen years old. His mother and stepfather must have received many of the leading politicians and generals at their house, and Plato may well have seen Alcibiades before his exile. Critias, Plato's cousin on his mother's side, was a prominent member of the Four Hundred, his sentiments being those of the moderate party led by Theramenes. As the author of numerous poems and political essays, he must have been regarded with special respect by Plato. But the pendulum had soon swung back to extreme democracy. Without the support of the fleet, collected at Samos, the Four Hundred were helpless; and those serving with the fleet were resolved to pursue the war with Sparta until victory had been gained. On their motion, Alcibiades was recalled and elected a general; but when a naval defeat was sustained in 407, he knew that his spell of power was over, and retired to his estates in the Chersonese. As for Critias, he seems to have been exiled after the collapse of the Four Hundred; we next hear of him encouraging an insurrection of slaves in Thessaly.

The Athenian empire had been the creation of democracy; Sparta, though highly aristocratic in her domestic government, had been able to announce that the cause for which she fought Athens was the freedom and independence of the Greeks. It was inevitable that when, in 404, Athens surrendered to Sparta and was deprived of her empire, she should submit also to some form of oligarchy. The exiles, including Critias, returned. Plato began to reflect about his own career [1] : should he plunge into this stormy sea of politics, and where should he bestow his sympathy? An easy answer was offered to him—his relatives Critias and Charmides, who were members of ' the Thirty ', invited him to join them. But Plato, perhaps owing to natural timidity, perhaps from the warning of Socrates, held back. Late in life he wrote that his youthful innocence was such that he hoped to see a new reign of justice. But his friends and kinsmen ' soon made the

[1] The Seventh Letter, which is now generally accepted as genuine, gives an account of Plato's attitude to practical politics. It describes his early disappointments, beginning with the institution of the Thirty, and tells the story of his three visits to Sicily.

earlier constitution seem like the Golden Age '. Arrests
and executions followed one another in rapid succession,
and, wishing to compromise all those who held moderate
views, the Thirty commanded several of them to arrest
innocent fellow-citizens ;   among these Socrates—whom
Plato simply describes as φίλον ἄνδρα ἐμοὶ πρεσβύτερον—
was ordered to carry out the arrest of Leon of Salamis.
He took no notice of the order, but before he could be
punished, the Thirty were overthrown.   Many of them,
including Critias and Charmides, died in the battle at the
Piraeus.

One of the first acts of the restored democracy was to
decree an ' amnesty ' for previous crimes and injustices :
' on that occasion,' writes Plato, ' those who returned
from exile behaved with great moderation.'   The hope of
a political career sprang up afresh in his mind, but he was
deterred by his youth, and by the absence of any party
of sympathetic friends.   Soon a crushing blow came. We
shall speak presently of the character and teaching of
Socrates, as his intimates knew him ; he aimed above all
at real knowledge, as opposed to pretence and persuasive-
ness, and, in order to emphasize this ideal, professed doubt
and ignorance.   But to the average Athenian he appeared
as a dogmatic teacher of the most dangerous and
demoralizing kind.   Some remembered how he had been
attacked by the comedians, twenty years before, for
' making the worse reason appear the better ' ; all were
accustomed to the sight of him in the gymnasium
apparently imparting his gospel to a group of innocent
young admirers—and it was known that two of these
admirers, in times past, had been Alcibiades and Critias.
It required no more to unleash the fury of the new
democracy, and at the age of seventy Socrates was faced
for the first time with a prosecution.   One clause, which
may have been deliberately vague on account of the

amnesty, accused him of exercising a corrupting influence upon the young men.[1] A small majority of the judges, found him guilty, and having neglected his chance to plead for a lighter punishment, he was sentenced, by a more decisive vote, to undergo death by hemlock. Plato had been present at the trial (cf. *Apology*, 34A, where Socrates names him as one whose relatives might have protested if they saw him being led astray) ; but he lay ill when Socrates drank the hemlock in the prison some weeks later.

[1] *Apology* 24B : Σωκράτη φησὶν ἀδικεῖν τούς τε νέους διαφθείροντα καὶ θεοὺς οὓς ἡ πόλις νομίζει οὐ νομίζοντα, ἕτερα δὲ δαιμόνια καινά. The precise meaning of the second accusation depends on the sense of νομίζειν. As far as we know, a man could not be prosecuted merely for heterodox opinions ; and οὐ νομίζοντα may mean ' not acknowledging' by joining in the established public worship. See Burnet *ad loc.*

II

What picture are we to form of Plato's early training? This question has a special interest, since Plato, though a conservative in many respects, nevertheless led the way in a great reform of education.

There was a traditional division of education into two branches—γυμναστική or physical training, and μουσική, the training of the mind and senses (*Republic*, 376ε). It is to be presumed that Plato as a boy partook in the usual athletic exercises, and later saw military service. His own schemes of education give great prominence to physical training, but only because a vigorous body is the basis of a vigorous character : γυμναστική, no less than μουσική, should serve to educate the soul (*Republic*, 410c). The idea of a *harmony* between soul and body was all-important to him, and he graphically describes the one-sided characters which may result from an excess of either gymnastic or musical training (*Republic*, 411α). From this point of view, he modified the Greek athleticism ; he had no wish to impose on everyone the severe régime under-taken by athletes in training for great feats, which, he remarked, was not necessarily conducive to general health (*Republic*, 404α). As to military exercises, though he takes their inclusion for granted, he finds fault with the Spartan education for placing undue emphasis upon them, and thus teaching courage to the neglect of the higher virtues (*Laws*, i, 629–30).

Similarly in regard to education in μουσική, Plato requires much that is new, but builds upon the old. The first thing which strikes us about this term, as used in the *Republic*, is its very wide extension : poetry and painting, science and philosophy, all came under the patronage of

the Muses, no less than singing and instrumental music.—
Plato begins at the very beginning, with the stories which
children will hear from their mothers and nurses. These
are bound to be fabulous—one cannot begin with the
unvarnished truth—but Plato insists that they should give
a true *impression*. Now many of the stories which Homer
and Hesiod tell about the Gods and heroes, and the life
which awaits men in the underworld, are unsuitable for
children to hear ; these passages must be censored, and
careful instructions given to future poets. Then there
must be rules for the *form* of literature, which may be as
dangerous as its matter : the dramatic form is especially
deplorable, as it leads to the tendency to imitate every
kind of model, irrespective of its worth. Here it is fitting
to emphasize a point in which Greek education differed
from our own. Oral instruction was the rule, not the
exception. Books were scarce, and not very convenient
in form ; one received the impression of words through
the ear, rather than through the eye. This led to a different
estimate of intellectual ability and Plato always gives a
high rank to memory among mental endowments ; and
he tells a story in the *Phaedrus* to show that the invention
of writing is not an unmixed blessing.

Plato's treatment of music, in the narrower sense, bears
witness to its importance in the education of his day.
Just as he prefers the narrative form in literature to the
dramatic, because it is simpler and more sincere, so
he selects certain melodies and rhythms as typical of
a calm and resolute character. Skill in music was perhaps
more universal in Greece than it is amongst ourselves ;
we hear from Aristotle (*Politics*, 1341A, 34) that until the
Persian Wars, and for some time later, most free men could
play the flute ; and Plato himself in the *Laws* assumes it
to be a natural thing for the whole population to take part
in choral singing.

It will naturally be asked if there was no *intellectual* training to stiffen this predominantly artistic education. Mathematics was not normally pursued beyond the stage of mere reckoning ; for Plato frequently denounces the prevailing state of ignorance, and strongly recommends mathematical study for its value as a discipline and its practical usefulness. Nor can we suppose that an interest in philosophy was in any way *normal* ; we hear that Plato himself ' associated with ' the Heraclitean philosopher Cratylus, but we cannot regard this as part of the normal education of an Athenian. It was just here that Plato found the essential weakness of the usual education—it trained the senses, and imparted ' right opinions ' about music and politics, but left the young man without any standard of accurate *knowledge*. And the same fact lies behind his criticism of a great educational movement of which we have still to speak—that of the Sophists who are represented in the *Republic* by Thrasymachus. These were teachers who imparted what appeared to be a general culture, but above all professed the arts of oratory and persuasion, in which lay the key to political success. We should not regard them as a sect professing some common doctrine, but as independent individuals. They all taught for profit ; they all professed universal knowledge ; they all made much of the opposition between φύσις and νόμος. Beyond this the similarity did not go : Thrasymachus scorned moral distinctions, whilst Gorgias was timidly conventional. Let us therefore glance at them separately.

Protagoras, of Abdera, paid his first visit to Athens in 444 B.C., when Pericles asked him to design a constitution for Thurii. He required fees for his teaching, and collected a great fortune from the various cities he visited. His book on ' Truth ' had a great circulation, and the mere news of his arrival at Athens caused a sensation among the young men. Man, declared Protagoras, is the measure of all things—of those that are, that they are, and of those that are not, that they are not. (He seems to have meant by this that every individual's perceptions are the standard of truth for him.) Protagoras also stressed the power of convention, νόμος, in human life ; νόμος, though opposed to φύσις, is a kind of second nature, from which man is unable to escape.

Gorgias of Leontini visited Athens in 427 B.C., at the age of sixty, as an ambassador of his native city. He impressed the Athenians chiefly as the exponent of a new kind of prose, full of precise antithesis and sparkling ornament. Plato, who must have known him in later years, does not give an unfavourable impression of him as a man, but makes him argue with some *naïveté* that even in the arts and sciences, rhetoric is superior to knowledge, because it is the practised orator, and not the specialist in a particular science, who can make people believe him. Gorgias also made an excursion into general philosophy. He maintained that, if strict accuracy is demanded, we know nothing—not even whether there is anything to know. This, of course, leaves the field clear for opinion and persuasion.

Hippias of Elis and Thrasymachus of Chalcedon belonged to a younger generation. Hippias claimed universal knowledge and artistic skill, and, if there is anything in Plato's caricature, liked to boast of the enormous profits he had earned. Thrasymachus, who was mentioned by Aristophanes as far back as 427 B.C., became famous both as an expert on the theory of style and as a practising orator. He excelled at arousing great audiences to a display of emotion, and could invent a calumny or dispose of it ' on any grounds or none ' (*Phaedrus*, 267E). More refined listeners called him ' the brawler ', making a pun on his name θρασυ-μαχος. He cared little for truth as such, and does not seem to have been a philosopher ; in order to exhibit his skill in debate he would defend unexpected 'paradoxes', until he could scarcely distinguish them from his true opinions (*Republic*, 346A).

Plato's complaint against the Sophists follows, as has been said, from his favourite contrast between knowledge and opinion. The Sophists had to adapt themselves to the opinions of the public from which they drew their fees. They encouraged the worship of success and happiness, and did nothing to refine the ideas which those words convey. Appearance was more vital to them than reality, persuasion than proof : it was from Socrates, whom the public regarded as a Sophist, that Plato learnt to formulate these objections.

Socrates, who was born about 470 B.C., had in his youth been deeply interested in scientific inquiry of the type practised by Empedocles and Anaxagoras. But, as he explains in a famous passage in the *Phaedo* (99A foll.), he could not be satisfied with any explanation of nature which ignored the factor of intelligence and design. To him it was not enough to learn that natural processes were governed by the shape and movement of material atoms— or that the primary elements of the world were Fire and Air, Earth and Water. Such science might show *how* a change took place, but could never give a reason *why* : it seemed to Socrates like a deaf man answering a question which had not been asked. From this followed a new idea of scientific method—science, being an investigation of *causes* in the sense just explained, must include not only observation through the senses, but argument and discussion (ἐν λόγοις σκοπεῖν τῶν πραγμάτων τὴν ἀλήθειαν) ; one must not only state the facts, but also frame a *hypothesis* which would account for them, and be ready to revise this hypothesis whenever it seemed necessary.

With these principles Socrates turned to the practical questions of human life. The philosopher finds men engaged, by common consent, in the pursuit of Happiness, but differing as to the path by which it may be reached. He finds that in every branch of activity there are experts in possession of special knowledge or skill, to whom a decision may be entrusted—the doctor, the shoemaker, and so on. Now this deference to authority ceases exactly where it would seem to be most desirable—i.e. where questions of justice and moral goodness are concerned. Every citizen decides for himself whether a law is just, or an enactment conducive to the good of the State. What is the explanation of this ? Are moral questions simply more difficult than these other questions, or are they different in kind ? In other words, is goodness an art dependent on some special training ? ' Yes,' an Athenian might answer, ' the Sophist claims to impart such a training, and to know what is τὸ εὖ ζῆν.' In several Dialogues—the *Protagoras, Gorgias, Meno, Euthydemus, Republic*—Plato shows us how Socrates was accustomed to examine this claim. The Sophist professes to teach ἀρετή. If it can be taught, as medicine or shoe-making can, it must be knowledge ; and it must be possible to give definitions (λόγοι, ὁρισμοί) of the virtues.. But the Sophists always fail in this elementary test. A Sophist, moreover, would have to allow that the very ἀρετή which he admired had been possessed to a high degree by Pericles and Themistocles, who were the most powerful statesmen of their time ; yet these great men had failed to hand on the precious secret to their sons. Nevertheless, it remained the deepest conviction of Socrates that virtue and knowledge were one. Reason and intellect must reign supreme in human life. And it is not difficult to see how this was reconciled with his argument against the Sophists : the highest imaginable political ἀρετή would necessarily involve philosophical insight into human nature ; but as in the arts, so in politics there is a kind of skill—not less efficient than knowledge in most of the circumstances of life—which comes to a man from long experience and practised intuition : it was this ἀρετή which the great statesmen of the past possessed, and it is this which the Sophist vainly professes to teach.

III

Either during the lifetime of Socrates, or shortly after his death, Plato began to write imaginary Socratic conversations and to publish them as literature. There is little doubt that Plato led the way, but he was followed later by Aeschines of Sphettus, Xenophon, and others, each of whom interpreted the character and teaching of Socrates in his own way. Plato never ceases to display a reserve and hesitation in writing, which are the result of his original rôle as a reporter of Socratic conversations. So long as he was mainly occupied with moral and practical questions, and this was for the greater part of his life, he retained Socrates as the leading figure, though it is not to be supposed that ' the historical Socrates ' could have said all that is attributed to him in a Dialogue like the *Republic* or *Cratylus*. Later, the influence of Eleatic and Pythagorean contemporaries turned Plato to new regions of thought—the study of nature, the analysis of language and judgment—and he gave the principal part to imaginary speakers, though, in all his Dialogues except the *Laws*, Socrates remained present as a spectator. He took less care to create a varied background for the Dialogues ; question and answer became more and more a barren formality ; and being no longer obliged to reproduce the speech of ordinary conversation, Plato tended to use recondite words and an artificial rhythm and construction. His later Dialogues, however, are not mere lectures, such as he might have given to his pupils in the Academy ; for, as we see in the *Phaedrus* (276D), he always drew a sharp distinction between literature and oral teaching. Strictly speaking, a book could not *teach*, for teaching involves

question and answer ; its highest purpose was to amuse
the reader in a salutary way, or, for the person who had
written it, to serve as a memorandum of his beliefs. It is
clear from the evidence of Aristotle, who was a member
of the Academy, that Plato was faithful to the principles
expressed in the *Phaedrus*, and never committed to writing
certain doctrines in which he profoundly believed.

Even the death of Socrates did not extinguish Plato's
practical aspirations, but it did destroy his faith in
democracy and make him regard the moral regeneration
of Athens as hopeless. He seems to have spent some years
at Megara, in company with the philosopher Euclides.
About 390 B.C., when he was thirty-seven years of age, he
set out on a long journey, first visiting Egypt, whose
traditions are often recalled in his writings, and afterwards
Cyrene, Italy, and Sicily. Cyrene was the home of a famous
mathematician, Theodorus, and it is not unreasonable to
suppose that Plato went there in order to make his
acquaintance. A similar motive lay behind his visit to
Southern Italy, for Tarentum was the home of the most
progressive and influential school of the day.   In the
sixth century, Pythagoras, emigrating from his home at
Samos, had settled at Croton and left behind him a
community of followers who led a kind of monastic life,
and professed a somewhat superstitious devotion to
mathematics.   But these old Pythagoreans engaged in
political intrigues which made them unpopular with their
neighbours, and they were disbanded. At some time in
Plato's youth a new school was established at Tarentum
by a man of exceptional genius, the scientist and statesman,
Archytas. It was likewise called Pythagorean, though it
may not itself have claimed this name. Under the
presidency of Archytas, it made astonishing progress in
mathematics and astronomy. The planets were probably
distinguished from the fixed stars at some time during the

fifth century,[1] but no general theory of their movement had yet been advanced; they were supposed to wander (πλανᾶσθαι) about the sky, whilst the Earth stood motionless at the centre of the Universe; and the fixed stars were thought to be luminous points on the inner side of a rotating hemisphere. The school of Archytas substituted for this a very modern hypothesis. In the first place they proved that the planets move in regular orbits; and this hypothesis implies a considerable number of observations, as well as great mathematical skill. Secondly they supposed that the Earth was not the centre of the Universe, but a spherical planet, moving around an invisible central Fire. Plato alludes to these theories in the myths appended to the *Phaedo* and *Republic*. At Tarentum he must have greatly extended his knowledge of mathematics, and it may be also that he now heard for the first time philosophical reasons for the belief in the immortality of the soul.[2] Add to this the fact that Archytas was the leading statesman of the city, and that he was elected seven times to the post of general, in defiance of a law which forbade re-election, and it is easy to imagine how deeply Plato was impressed. He says in the Seventh Letter that at the time of this journey his own experience had convinced him that until cities were ruled by philosophers, the human race would never fare better than in the past.

Plato's adventures in Sicily belong to a different chapter of his life, and we will here follow him back to Athens. He

[1] The names Jupiter, Saturn and Mars occur in Greek form in the *Epinomis* (986 *e* 7), for the first time in European literature; but it seems to be implied there that they had long been current, at least among philosophers and scientists.

[2] This statement does not rest on his own evidence, but on that of Cicero (*de Finibus*, v, 87; *de Republica*, i, 10), who attributes the whole speculative side of Plato's philosophy to his contact with the Pythagoreans. Thus, says Cicero, Plato had to represent *Socrates* as expounding *numeros et geometriam et harmoniam . . . Pythagorae more.* (See G. C. Field, *Plato and His Contemporaries*, pp. 15, 223.)

established, in or near a gymnasium called the *Academy*, a school which remained his chief concern for the rest of his life, and survived for eight centuries after his death. The Academy was legally a religious body (θίασος), sacred to the Muses. It bore a strong family resemblance to the modern college ; there were lectures (ἀκροάσεις or συνουσίαι) by Plato and other leading members of the school ; all kinds of research were pursued, including the study of animals and plants ; eminent strangers, like the Sicilian doctor, Philistion, or the astronomer Eudoxus, stayed in the school. But although it was a home of research, the Academy included a great many who were destined to return to their native cities as legislators or politicians, and this must have been very satisfactory to Plato himself. He did not found the Academy as a place of retirement from active life. He thought that the pursuit of truth was necessarily connected with the reform of human conduct.

In his view, the defect of Athenian culture, as it existed in the Periclean age, was that it was not founded upon knowledge, and so had nowhere to turn in a time of crisis. It was cemented by habit and custom, rather than by knowledge, and when put to the test, could not ' give an account of itself ', a point which is excellently brought out by the example of Polemarchus and his father in Book I of the *Republic*. In contrast to this, Plato wished to see human institutions founded on a rational basis, which would be thoroughly understood by those who had to manage them. He therefore recommended mathematical discipline as a preparation for active life, and enforced it in his Academy. This brought much criticism upon him from his rival and predecessor Isocrates, and from the comedians. Now, of course, Plato did not believe that particular problems could by solved by mathematical deduction. But he argued that knowledge was always the same, whether applied to practice or not. If human emotions, for instance, were properly understood and classified, how powerful Rhetoric could be! And again, just as the truth of mathematics is one, is there not the same standard of Justice and Beauty for all times and places? Such standards, called Ideas, were and have always remained the central feature of the philosophy of Plato. He held their existence to be far more certain than that of particular things and actions in the familiar world [1]; for these things and actions can only give rise to opinions, whereas in moral experience and in mathematics we are introduced to the realm of knowledge. Plato constantly adapted this belief to new regions of study, and made experiments with new methods, but his conviction of the reality of Ideas, and of the essential difference between knowledge and sense-perception, never deserted him. When the Academy abandoned the belief in Ideas, a few generations after his death, it became a school of Scepticism.

[1] It should be remembered that Plato, so far as he held any belief at first about the nature of the physical world, accepted from his Heraclitean friend Cratylus the view that there are no permanent physical substances, but only movements and changes.

IV

The two principal actors in Book I have already been mentioned here : we must next glance at the minor characters, and first, since the scene is laid at their house, at Cephalus and his sons.

We learn the history of the family from a speech afterwards composed by Lysias, the $Kaτ'$ $'Eρατοσθένους$. Cephalus, a Syracusan by birth, came to Athens on the invitation of Pericles ; he lived there as a $μέτοικος$ (resident alien) for thirty years ; during all this time no member of the family had occasion to appear in a court of law, either as plaintiff or as defendant ; and Cephalus, though not an Athenian citizen, had often undertaken the $λειτούργιαι$ which were expected from the wealthy. This did not save his sons from ruin during the tyranny of the Thirty. On some pretext of disloyalty, orders were issued for the arrest of Lysias and Polemarchus, and the confiscation of their property. Lysias managed to bribe his captor, and to escape with his life, but Polemarchus was thrown into prison, where he ' received the usual command, to drink the hemlock '. Meanwhile the source of their wealth, a shield-factory at which one hundred and twenty slaves were employed, was occupied and confiscated ; Lysias even alleges that the wife of Polemarchus was forced to give up her ear-rings. Lysias returned when the democracy was restored, and was able to bring Eratosthenes, one of the Thirty, to justice for the murder of his brother. (The Thirty themselves were excluded from the ' amnesty ' declared at the time of the restoration.)

Plato brings us back to the lifetime of Cephalus. Lysias is still a young student of rhetoric (it is, no doubt, he who has invited Thrasymachus to the house) ; Cephalus is extremely old, and may have retired from business, but has not actually handed over his wealth to his sons. (See notes on 328B, 330B.)   In the *Phaedrus* Socrates mentions Polemarchus as one who has devoted his attention to philosophy, and hopes that Lysias may be brought to do the same.

Other characters in the *Republic* are Plato's elder brothers, Glaucon and Adeimantus—who are inconspicuous in Book I only because they have a great part to play in the next book—Charmantides and Cleitophon, who are mere names to us, but may be inferred to be Athenian admirers of Thrasymachus ; and Niceratus, a son of the famous Nicias.   We hear of Niceratus again from Xenophon (*Sympos.*, iii, 5), who says that his father made him learn the *Iliad* and *Odyssey* by heart.   Like Polemarchus, he fell a victim to the Thirty ; there are, in fact, three persons present at the Dialogue who had drunk the hemlock when Plato wrote, but it is characteristic of him not to use this to stir up an irrelevant emotion.

(b) THE DRAMATIC DATE

It is natural also to ask whether Plato envisages a definite date for the occurrence of the conversation.   This is a question which has given rise to much discussion.   It is by no means agreed that Plato observed any principle about chronology ; some, like Jowett, prefer to regard him as a writer of fiction who did not care for historical accuracy. Apart from this dispute, which concerns a general principle, there is some difficulty in the choice of any definite date for this particular conversation.

The occasion is the first festival to be held at the Piraeus in honour of Bendis (327A, cf. 354A), but there is no independent evidence to show when this was.   Cephalus is in extreme old age ; Thrasymachus, at the height of his fame ; and Socrates, to judge from general appearances, a middle-aged man. Glaucon and Adeimantus give an impression of youth, but it appears from ii, 368A, that they are old enough to have distinguished themselves in a battle. There is an incidental allusion, which it would be rash to use for purposes of chronology, to the athlete Polydamas (338C), who is reported to have gained a victory in 408 B.C. ; and there is one obvious anachronism, the mention of Ismenias (336A), whose misdeeds did not begin until after the death of Socrates (see note on p. 92).

Among these data the most reliable are those provided by the ages of Cephalus, Thrasymachus, and Socrates. We shall do well to accept the suggestion of A. E. Taylor (*Plato, the Man and his Work*, p. 264), that ' the supposed date of the conversation must be about the time of the peace of Nicias (spring, 421 B.C.), certainly not later. It is important to remember that Athens came out of the Archidamian War at that date, though not quite on the terms she might have got, but for the folly of the democratic leaders, four years earlier, still far and away the richest and most powerful of the combatant states, with the main of her empire intact '. (Some scholars have attempted to argue, on the evidence of an anonymous *Life of Lysias*, that at such a date Cephalus and his sons could not have been in residence at the Piraeus ; but the evidence does not bear a close scrutiny. It tells us (1) that Lysias's father died when he was a youth of fifteen, (2) that he then settled at the colony of Thurii, which had just been founded (in 444 B.C.), and returned to Athens, now a successful orator, in 411. The view has therefore been held that the supposed date of the *Republic* must come later than 411, Cephalus being brought back to life. But this is to pay too much respect to the imaginings of a late and anonymous biographer. It seems to be true that Lysias visited Thurii, but not that he went there as one of the first colonists and remained for a great part of his life. Again, he himself claims that

Cephalus was invited to come to Athens by Pericles, and lived there for thirty years ; and this makes it impossible that Cephalus can have died as soon as 444.)

The dramatic date of the *Republic* is sometimes considered by scholars in connection with that of the *Timaeus*. They hold that the narrative of the *Republic* and the dialogue of the *Timaeus* take place on successive days, but this is probably a mistake : for details see Cornford, *Plato's Cosmology*, p. 4.

V

It is not the definition of Justice—says Socrates to the
departing Cephalus—to speak the truth, and to restore what
one has received. Surely it is ! says Polemarchus, and one
may learn this from Simonides : he says it is just to pay
what one owes to every man, and seems to me to speak well.

Polemarchus's failure to make good his case is due,
partly to the fact that he does not see the difference between
an instance of Justice and a statement of its general nature,
and partly to the fact that he always allows the argument
to take a wrong turning. He is led to see that Justice,
being ἀνθρωπεία ἀρετή, cannot be used in order to harm
one's enemies, and to this extent a positive result is reached ;
but this result is not worth much after all the chances which
have been missed.

Is it always just to restore deposits ? Consider the case
of a man who deposits arms with a friend, and claims them
again when he is no longer of sound mind. ' Simonides may
have meant that one always owes good to one's friends and
evil to one's enemies.' By ὀφειλόμενον, in fact, he meant
προσῆκον (what is fitting). (This change considerably
weakens the position of Polemarchus. The plausibility of
his first formula lay in the fact that it reproduced the notion
of a debt or obligation, which is essential to Justice.) Now
the art of medicine renders what is fitting to those in
sickness (and so on, with further instances) : where, and
to whom, does Justice render what is fitting ? ' In forming
alliances, and in the conduct of wars.' But the doctor is
useless to those who are not sick, the steersman to those who
are not at sea : is the just man useless to those who are not
at war ? ' He has his use in peace : he helps in contracts

and partnerships.'   But in playing chess we seek the
partnership of the chess-player (again fresh instances may
be supplied) : on what occasion do we prefer the partnership of the just man ?   ' Where money is at stake.'   But
not where it is to be used : in buying a ship or a horse,
we should want the advice of one who knows about ships
or horses.   ' The just man is useful where money has to be
deposited and kept safe.'   And is this true of all other
articles—a shield, a lyre, a pruning-hook ?   The just man
does not teach how to use things, but how to guard them ?
' Apparently.'   Justice, then, is not a very serious sort of
thing : wherever we look, it is ' useless in use, and useful
only in disuse ' (331D–333E).

From these consequences Polemarchus could have
escaped, broadly speaking, in either of two ways : he
could have stated firmly that it was in no sense a kind of
knowledge focused on a special object, i.e. he could have
refused to admit the analogy of the arts : or, allowing it
to be comparable to an art, he could have said that it
exercised a regulative function in respect to the other arts,
and therefore had no special province of its own.   It is its
business, he might have said, to provide and maintain the
framework of society, and though it seems to be useless in
comparison with the arts, it is really far more useful than
they, because it provides peace, leisure, and a general
expectation of honest behaviour, without which no art
could ever be developed.   A modern thinker, suspicious
of anything which seems to assimilate the moral attitude
to the technical, would probably choose the first form of
statement : but Plato, as we may infer from later books,
chooses, and thinks Polemarchus should have chosen, the
second.   This should be remembered also in connection
with the argument with Thrasymachus.

But the man who can most effectively strike a blow, or
inflict an injury, is also best able to protect himself against

it (φυλάξασθαι). The soldier who can guard his own camp knows best how to elude the guard of the enemy ; one who is used to deceive, can best take care not to be deceived. But the just man is a skilful guardian of money ; hence he is also a skilful thief (333E–334B).

Three observations may be made on this strange argument. (1) Polemarchus might have quoted many examples in which we recognize that the art of defence differs from that of attack ; though it is probable that, the nearer an art comes to scientific accuracy, the truer it is that it is similarly related to opposites. (2) The term 'a skilful thief' (δεινὸς φυλάττειν, δεινὸς κλέπτειν) is misleading. We are not concerned with a branch of knowledge, but with a state of character. Δεινός suggests (a) able to steal, and (b) fond of stealing. Socrates mischievously substitutes (b) for (a). (3) There is also, when we look closely, a play on the words φυλάττειν and φυλάξασθαι. As used by Polemarchus, φυλάττειν meant 'keep', 'guard'. Socrates confuses him by mentioning a case where we 'guard against', or ward off, an injury (φυλάξασθαι), and with reference to this, shows that the art of defence is the same as the art of attack. Then, by means of the phrase στρατοπέδου φύλαξ, 'guard of the camp,' we return to φυλάττειν once more, and it is proved that the clever guardian is the clever thief.

The argument enters upon a new phase. One's friends and enemies, who are they ? They are those who are good or bad to us, χρηστοί or πονηροί. Does this mean those whom we judge to be good or bad, or those who really are so, whether we think so or not ? The former, says Polemarchus. But where we are deceived by appearances, and take our true friend for an enemy, it will be just, according to the formula we are considering, to do harm to him ; and likewise we must assist our real enemy. It is just to harm those who are guilty of no injustice. Impossible !

exclaims Polemarchus—it must be just to harm those who are unjust, but to assist those who are just. But how does a man know who deserve these names? Again, by his own fallible judgment. So he will now sometimes do harm to his true friends, and good to his true enemies. ' But let us retrace our steps : let us define a friend, not as one who appears to be, but as one who both appears to be and is, χρηστός ; and an enemy accordingly.' But can it, even in this sense, be the part of a just man to injure his enemies ? To harm or injure a horse, is to take away from its worth or value as a horse ; to harm another man, is to deprive him of worth as a man—it is *to make him worse*. But Justice is virtue, it *is* human worth or value. To say that it is the function of Justice to harm another man, is like saying that it is the function of Music to make him unmusical, or of heat to make him cold (334c–336A). (The fallacy in this may be expressed as follows. In the moral sense of the word *injure*, which is in question when Polemarchus speaks of a harm or injury to one's enemies, there is no implication that another *person* is made worse. It is his possessions, or his life and liberty, that are adversely affected ; and *he* is injured through them. It is different where we speak of an injury to one's horse, or one's watch, or one's collar-bone ; in all these cases the thing is injured, βλάπτεται, by becoming less efficient for a purpose.)

The argument with Polemarchus is followed by an interlude (336D–338B), in which we begin to see the character of Thrasymachus. Leave this nauseating polite-ness, he insists, and ' tell me clearly and accurately (σαφῶς καὶ ἀκριβῶς, 336D), what you consider Justice to be ; and take care not to tell me that it is the obligatory, or the advantageous, or the profitable, for I am not the sort of person to be put off with rubbish like that.' What answer is he himself prepared to give ? ' Justice, I say, is nothing but the advantage of the stronger? (or superior, τοῦ κρείττονος,

338c).' What does this mean? Polydamas the boxer and wrestler is strong, but—' I mean by the stronger those who make the laws in cities, i.e. either the tyrant, the democracy, or the aristocracy. The ruler, being the ruler, is stronger (κρατεῖ, κρεῖττον ἐστιν) ; in making the laws, he looks to his own interest ; it is just for the subjects to obey the laws ; therefore it is just for them to act in the interest of the stronger.' But this position is inconsistent. The judgment of a ruler is fallible, and so he may make a law which is disadvantageous to himself ; a law which it will be just for his subjects to obey. ' No,' says Cleitophon, interposing on behalf of Thrasymachus, ' for it was understood that " the advantage of the stronger " meant anything which he himself *thought* to be advantageous.' But Thrasymachus does not accept the suggestion. ' The idea that a ruler can make a mistake, he says, is inaccurate nonsense. Art or science, so long as it is art or science, leads nobody astray ; it is always true, or it would not be entited to the name. Doubtless we find it convenient to say that " this doctor, or this accountant, has made a mistake ". But in such cases it is not the doctor, but the fallible human being who is normally a doctor, who is wrong. In accurate speech (notice this reiterated demand for ἀκρίβεια), we ought not to say that a *ruler* could choose a law which failed to promote his own interest ' (338c–341A).

There are two noticeable points of contrast between this argument and the preceding one. Firstly, Thrasymachus, unlike Polemarchus, knows what is meant by a definition, and strives to include the whole of Justice in a general formula. Secondly he himself, without waiting for a suggestion from Socrates, introduces the notion of ruling as an art, and insists that it shall be applied in a spirit of ἀκρίβεια. And this gives us, in miniature, a historical truth : it was part of the profession of the Sophists that government was an art, to which they possessed the key.

Socrates accepted the equation, but exposed their pretension to the art as a false one, and did not pretend to have it himself.

So far Thrasymachus has escaped from criticism, but not without a sacrifice. He intended to offer a sturdy realistic view, which had the courage to look facts in the face, and would not be deceived by fine names. Almost at once he has had to take refuge in a remote Utopia, inhabited by impeccable artists. His distinction cannot possibly be of any practical use ; a man may, no doubt, encourage himself by the thought that the science of medicine, as such, is perfect, but when he is ill, he must go to a doctor who is liable to make mistakes ; the doctor himself cannot warn him when these mistakes are coming ; and this means that the arts as we know them, are fallible.

Socrates, displaying genuine skill in argument for the first time, proceeds to draw a new corollary from the notion of a perfect art. No art attends to its own welfare ; there is always an object, such as the human body, over which the art presides, and whilst the art consciously seeks the welfare of the object, it unconsciously achieves its own welfare. The body is liable to unsoundness, πονηρία, and without the help of medical science, cannot be assured of its ἀρετή, health ; but medical science is not liable to unsoundness. If it were, we should need to look for some new art, which might serve as a kind of medicine of medicine ; and we should be led gradually into an infinite regress.

Thus an art has no welfare or advantage which can be distinguished from the welfare of the object committed to its care. (True, we say that the medical profession is profitable, or is a way of making money. Socrates's view of this appears at a later stage. The function of the doctor *as such* is to promote and preserve health ; the profits which a man obtains as a doctor are not the (direct) consequence of his skill in that capacity ; they come from the fact that he exercises the art of money-making as well.) We are now driven to the conclusion that the art of ruling in the accurate sense—and Thrasymachus insists on accuracy—is entirely concerned in promoting the welfare of the subjects ruled (341B–342E).

This argument, though its use in the debate is highly ingenious, is not really valid. The relation between the art and the object is not always what it is in the special instance of medicine. Every art has an object, but there is no guarantee that every art seeks the good of its object, and if it does, this may be because it coincides with the good of the artist. De Quincey once imagined that murder might be included among the fine arts. Not to take so extreme an instance, we may point out that the art of tennis consists in striking the ball, which does not do the ball either good or harm ; and the art of gardening is, it is true, interested in the health of vegetables, but it does not—as Socrates would pretend—grow vegetables in their own interest. Even as a gardener, the gardener knows that he grows vegetables for use and profit. This is a point afterwards made by Thrasymachus.

After some violent abuse, Thrasymachus now delivers a long speech. Socrates, he says somewhat incongruously, is a hopeless idealist. He thinks that the shepherd fattens the sheep for their own good, not for that of the farmer. And he thinks, in spite of obvious facts, that the governing classes in cities neglect their own interest, and are solicitous only for the welfare of their subjects. The truth is that Justice is always personal loss, and someone else's gain (οἰκεία βλαβή, ἀλλότριον ἀγαθόν). Whenever the just man is in partnership with the unjust, he comes off worst ; when the State collects taxes or distributes profits, he is cheated ; when he is appointed to office, the just man makes sacrifices, whilst the unjust man enriches himself. Whence comes the universal hatred and abuse of injustice ?

Simply from this, that dishonesty on a small scale is to the general disadvantage, and everyone professes to hate it ; the real feelings of men are seen when a supremely strong man triumphs over the forces of opinion and practises injustice in its most complete form, injustice against the whole State, i.e. in successful tyranny. What was formerly abused is now the subject of flattery and admiration. This flattery tells its own tale.   Men covet the power of a tyrant, but feeling themselves weak and liable to suffer if there were no restraint of law, they do not dare openly to admire injustice.   In reality injustice is stronger and more worthy of a free man than justice, and injustice is what is profitable to oneself, whereas justice is the advantage of the stronger or superior (τοῦ κρείττονος). (343B–334B.)

The speech is too rhetorical, too rambling to make for success in the present debate.   Its principal defects are two.   The first I have tried to explain in the note on 334C 7 : Thrasymachus, instead of consistently maintaining that might is right and that whatever law the strong impose is *ipso facto* just, reintroduces the idea of justice in its conventional sense and now denounces it as a form of weakness.   The trouble is that he once more fails to maintain his profession of realism : his original case was that, once the veil of hypocrisy has been removed, it would appear that justice is simply power : and the logical consequence of this is that a tyrant is not a very unjust man, but on the contrary a very just one. Thrasymachus, it seems, hesitates to say this and offers quite a different account of the meaning of Justice—i.e. that the multitude of weak men combine together in order to safeguard themselves against the aggression of the superman, and that the law which *they* impose is Justice. This is a good example of the danger which attends any attempt to reverse the meaning of ethical terms.   Ethics is like science in being an attempt to find order and system amid apparently unrelated facts ; it is unlike science in having for its material the judgments and opinions of common men. It must take this material as it is, and may not alter it for the sake of a neat generalization.

The second defect in the speech is that it raises a new issue without recognizing its novelty, for it was not part of the original contention that Injustice is in itself more desirable and stronger than Justice. (See the remarks of Socrates, 347E 3, 354B.) But since he has now decided to say that the strong man is *unjust*, Thrasymachus is naturally led to say whatever he can in praise of Injustice.

The remainder of the argument has therefore a two-fold purpose : first, to overthrow the definition of Justice as τὸ τοῦ κρείττονος συμφέρον (344D–347E), and secondly to show that strength and happiness are not associated with Injustice, but with Justice (348B–354C). On the first point, Socrates asks what has happened to the demand for ἀκρίβεια? It had been shown that every art τῷ ἀκριβεῖ λόγῳ must consider the welfare of its object. Either ruling is for the benefit of those ruled, or it is not an art. Thrasymachus has failed to make a necessary distinction. It is always *possible* to obtain money or profits in the exercise of one's art. But no art can have two objects ; no man, in the same capacity, can aim simultaneously at two different ends. It is incorrect, then, to speak of a profit derived " from " medicine or shoe-making ; the shoes are derived from shoe-making, but the profit from the art of profit or wages, μισθαρνητική or μισθωτικὴ τέχνη. Similarly any personal gains which a man obtains from the exercise of political rule are the gains of the profit-maker, not of the politician. If ever there were a community of good men, they would not compete in order to rule, but in order to escape ruling. The best men would only rule when special persuasion had been brought to bear on them—not necessarily the offer of money or honour, but perhaps the dislike of being ruled by someone more incompetent than themselves.

It has already been said that the argument used by Socrates cannot prove that every art strives for the *advantage* of its object ; and this criticism still applies. Thrasymachus, though he labours under a confusion of his own, is quite right to point out that the art of tending sheep is a contrary instance which disproves Socrates's notion of τέχνη. The idea that profit-making is itself an art does not meet this criticism, and is not a correct representation of the motives of those who work for profit. (In the note on 346B I have tried to show that if we regard the μισθαρνητικὴ τέχνη as an accompaniment of *all* profitable use of art, we can no longer distinguish between a case in which art is employed *for the sake of* profit, and one in which the profit accidentally follows, though it was neither foreseen nor desired.)

It remains to consider the view, to which Thrasymachus passed during the course of his speech, that men universally admire Injustice, knowing it to be a source of strength, of happiness, and of freedom. A further twofold division is convenient. (1) Socrates shows that the properties which, in other spheres, we associate with prudence and virtue, belong to Justice rather than to Injustice (348B–352C). (2) Secondly, he infers from the view of the soul as the guiding principle in human nature, and from the fact that δικαιοσύνη is the virtue of the soul, that a just man or community is likely to be strong and happy.

Thrasymachus has identified Injustice with wisdom (εὐβουλία) and Justice with stupidity (εὐήθεια). Will he say that the first is ἀρετή and the second κακία ? He seems ready to do so, in all but the actual names. But it may be shown in the following way that the features of Injustice are those which characterize inexperience and ignorance. (1) Whatever others succeed in doing, whether they are unjust, like himself, or not, the unjust man tries to do something better. A just man, however, may try to ' get the advantage ' of an unjust rival, but knows that he cannot do better than another just man. (The whole argument depends on a vague use of πλεονεκτεῖν in the Greek. It is (a) to surpass, to do an action which *contains more goodness*, (b) to ' do better than ' a rival in the sense of vulgar competition ; to take unfair advantage of him, to gain profit at his expense.) (2) If you have a certain quality, you tend to resemble others who have the same quality. Now *ex hypothesi* the unjust man has σοφία and ἀρετή. He ought therefore to resemble others who have these qualities. (3) Turn now to σοφία and ἀρετή in the arts ; the ' knowing ' man (ἐπιστήμων), the skilled artist, knows that he cannot do better than another skilled artist but, at the most, do equally well. A musician cannot tune a lyre ' better ' than another musician ; if it is in tune the limit has been reached. But it would be quite characteristic of an unskilled man to engage in vain and boastful competition. (4) Injustice is therefore unwisdom, Justice wisdom and virtue. (For comment on this argument, see the notes.)

Again, it was claimed that strength necessarily went with Injustice. Has not this already been disproved—for knowledge, not ignorance, brings power ? But a more definite reason is this : it is the function of Justice to produce unanimity and harmony, of Injustice to produce division and discord. In the individual and in the commonwealth, among free men and among slaves, Injustice will make resolute and united action impossible. Nor can we argue that unjust men are often resolute ; communities of unjust men, such as bands of thieves, if they achieve success, do so in virtue of a remnant of Justice. (As to the individual, Plato had shown in the *Gorgias* that the more unjust a man is, the further he is from freedom ; the most unjust of all, a powerful tyrant, is ' free ' to obey all his

natural instincts, but for this reason never obeys himself.)
Thus an unjust man is at peace with nobody—neither
with the Gods, nor with men, nor with himself.

So we pass, on a tone noticeably graver than that which
has dominated the earlier argument, to a concluding proof
(352D foll.). It was said that ἄμεινον ζῶσιν οἱ δίκαιοι
τῶν ἀδίκων καὶ εὐδαιμονέστεροί εἰσιν. But every
existing thing, every being natural and artificial, is designed
for a purpose, ἔργον. That is its purpose or function
which it alone, or it in preference to other things, is suited
to perform : seeing, of the eyes, hearing, of the ear, and
so forth. Thus the soul has a unique and definite function,
which is to deliberate, to rule over the body and to impart
life ; (for all things which have life, even plants, are in
Greek ἔμψυχα). In order, then, to live well, a man requires
the excellence, ἀρετή, of the soul ; he requires Justice.
With Justice he will be blessed and happy (μακάριός τε
καὶ εὐδαίμων), without it, unfortunate and miserable.
Thus the claim of Thrasymachus has been answered, and
yet a satisfactory result has not been reached. Socrates
has tasted each dish as it was brought in to the banquet,
but has not given himself time to enjoy any of them.
Before learning what Justice really is, he has tried to prove
that it is better and more profitable than Injustice.

The final argument deserves great respect and attention,
for it expresses, perhaps in a somewhat hypothetical form,
cardinal doctrines of Plato which he preached to the end
of his life, and transmitted to Aristotle after him. The
mind or soul is not the servant of the passions, but is set
in authority over them. Thrasymachus starts from a false
contrast between the freedom of nature and the rule of
law. In reality Justice, self-control, and virtue are in
accordance with nature ; the city which displays them
will be most truly free ; the man who possesses them will
achieve his true destiny.

ΠΟΛΙΤΕΙΑ

Α

ΣΩΚΡΑΤΗΣ

p. 327

a Κατέβην χθὲς εἰς Πειραιᾶ μετὰ Γλαύκωνος τοῦ
Ἀρίστωνος προσευξόμενός τε τῇ θεῷ καὶ ἅμα τὴν
ἑορτὴν βουλόμενος θεάσασθαι τίνα τρόπον ποιήσουσιν
ἅτε νῦν πρῶτον ἄγοντες. καλὴ μὲν οὖν μοι καὶ ἡ τῶν
5 ἐπιχωρίων πομπὴ ἔδοξεν εἶναι, οὐ μέντοι ἧττον
ἐφαίνετο πρέπειν ἣν οἱ Θρᾷκες ἔπεμπον. προσευξάμενοι
b δὲ καὶ θεωρήσαντες ἀπῆμεν πρὸς τὸ ἄστυ. κατιδὼν
οὖν πόρρωθεν ἡμᾶς οἴκαδε ὡρμημένους Πολέμαρχος
ὁ Κεφάλου ἐκέλευσε δραμόντα τὸν παῖδα περιμεῖναί ἑ
κελεῦσαι. καί μου ὄπισθεν ὁ παῖς λαβόμενος τοῦ
5 ἱματίου, Κελεύει ὑμᾶς, ἔφη, Πολέμαρχος περιμεῖναι.
Καὶ ἐγὼ μετεστράφην τε καὶ ἠρόμην ὅπου αὐτὸς εἴη.
Οὗτος, ἔφη, ὄπισθεν προσέρχεται· ἀλλὰ περιμένετε.
Ἀλλὰ περιμενοῦμεν, ἦ δ' ὃς ὁ Γλαύκων.

c Καὶ ὀλίγῳ ὕστερον ὅ τε Πολέμαρχος ἧκε καὶ
Ἀδείμαντος ὁ τοῦ Γλαύκωνος ἀδελφὸς καὶ Νικήρατος
ὁ Νικίου καὶ ἄλλοι τινὲς ὡς ἀπὸ τῆς πομπῆς.

Ὁ οὖν Πολέμαρχος ἔφη· Ὦ Σώκρατες, δοκεῖτέ
5 μοι πρὸς ἄστυ ὡρμῆσθαι ὡς ἀπιόντες.

Οὐ γὰρ κακῶς δοξάζεις, ἦν δ' ἐγώ.

Ὁρᾷς οὖν ἡμᾶς, ἔφη, ὅσοι ἐσμέν ;

Πῶς γὰρ οὔ ;

Ἢ τοίνυν τούτων, ἔφη, κρείττους γένεσθε ἢ μένετ'
10 αὐτοῦ.

Οὐκοῦν, ἦν δ' ἐγώ, ἔτι ἐν λείπεται, τὸ ἦν πείσωμεν
ὑμᾶς ὡς χρὴ ἡμᾶς ἀφεῖναι ;

Ἦ καὶ δύναισθ' ἄν, ἦ δ' ὅς, πεῖσαι μὴ ἀκούοντας ; ←

Οὐδαμῶς, ἔφη ὁ Γλαύκων.

Ὡς τοίνυν μὴ ἀκουσομένων, οὕτω διανοεῖσθε.   15

Καὶ ὁ Ἀδείμαντος, Ἀρά γε, ἦ δ' ὅς, οὐδ' ἴστε ὅτι 328
λαμπὰς ἔσται πρὸς ἑσπέραν ἀφ' ἵππων τῇ θεῷ ;

Ἀφ' ἵππων ; ἦν δ' ἐγώ· καινόν γε τοῦτο. λαμπάδια
ἔχοντες διαδώσουσιν ἀλλήλοις ἀμιλλώμενοι τοῖς ἵπποις ;
ἢ πῶς λέγεις ;   5

Οὕτως, ἔφη ὁ Πολέμαρχος. καὶ πρός γε παννυχίδα
ποιήσουσιν, ἢν ἄξιον θεάσασθαι· ἐξαναστησόμεθα γὰρ
μετὰ τὸ δεῖπνον καὶ τὴν παννυχίδα θεασόμεθα. καὶ
συνεσόμεθά τε πολλοῖς τῶν νέων αὐτόθι καὶ δια-
λεξόμεθα. ἀλλὰ μένετε καὶ μὴ ἄλλως ποιεῖτε.   10

Καὶ ὁ Γλαύκων, Ἔοικεν, ἔφη, μενετέον εἶναι.   b

Ἀλλ' εἰ δοκεῖ, ἦν δ' ἐγώ, οὕτω χρὴ ποιεῖν.

Ἦιμεν οὖν οἴκαδε εἰς τοῦ Πολεμάρχου, καὶ Λυσίαν
τε αὐτόθι κατελάβομεν καὶ Εὐθύδημον, τοὺς τοῦ
Πολεμάρχου ἀδελφούς, καὶ δὴ καὶ Θρασύμαχον τὸν 5
Καλχηδόνιον καὶ Χαρμαντίδην τὸν Παιανιᾶ καὶ
Κλειτοφῶντα τὸν Ἀριστωνύμου· ἦν δ' ἔνδον καὶ ὁ
πατὴρ ὁ τοῦ Πολεμάρχου Κέφαλος. καὶ μάλα πρεσβύτης μοι ἔδοξεν εἶναι· διὰ χρόνου γὰρ καὶ ἑωράκη c
αὐτόν. καθῆστο δὲ ἐστεφανωμένος ἐπί τινος προσ-
κεφαλαίου τε καὶ δίφρου· τεθυκὼς γὰρ ἐτύγχανεν ἐν
τῇ αὐλῇ. ἐκαθεζόμεθα οὖν παρ' αὐτόν· ἔκειντο γὰρ
δίφροι τινὲς αὐτόθι κύκλῳ.   5

Εὐθὺς οὖν με ἰδὼν ὁ Κέφαλος ἠσπάζετό τε καὶ
εἶπεν· Ὦ Σώκρατες, οὐδὲ θαμίζεις ἡμῖν καταβαίνων
εἰς τὸν Πειραιᾶ. χρῆν μέντοι. εἰ μὲν γὰρ ἐγὼ ἔτι ἐν
δυνάμει ἦ τοῦ ῥᾳδίως πορεύεσθαι πρὸς τὸ ἄστυ,

d οὐδὲν ἂν σὲ ἔδει δεῦρο ἰέναι, ἀλλ' ἡμεῖς ἂν παρὰ σὲ
ἦμεν· νῦν δέ σε χρὴ πυκνότερον δεῦρο ἰέναι. ὡς εὖ
ἴσθι ὅτι ἔμοιγε ὅσον αἱ ἄλλαι αἱ κατὰ τὸ σῶμα
ἡδοναὶ ἀπομαραίνονται, τοσοῦτον αὔξονται αἱ περὶ
5 τούς λόγους ἐπιθυμίαι τε καὶ ἡδοναί. μὴ οὖν ἄλλως
ποίει, ἀλλὰ τοῖσδέ τε τοῖς νεανίσκοις σύνισθι καὶ
δεῦρο παρ' ἡμᾶς φοίτα ὡς παρὰ φίλους τε καὶ πάνυ
οἰκείους.

Καὶ μήν, ἦν δ' ἐγώ, ὦ Κέφαλε, χαίρω γε διαλεγόμενος
e τοῖς σφόδρα πρεσβύταις· δοκεῖ γάρ μοι χρῆναι παρ'
αὐτῶν πυνθάνεσθαι, ὥσπερ τινὰ ὁδὸν προεληλυθότων
ἣν καὶ ἡμᾶς ἴσως δεήσει πορεύεσθαι, ποία τίς ἐστιν,
τραχεῖα καὶ χαλεπή, ἢ ῥᾳδία καὶ εὔπορος. καὶ δὴ καὶ
5 σοῦ ἡδέως ἂν πυθοίμην ὅτι σοι φαίνεται τοῦτο, ἐπειδὴ
ἐνταῦθα ἤδη εἶ τῆς ἡλικίας ὃ δὴ " ἐπὶ γήραος οὐδῷ "
φασιν εἶναι οἱ ποιηταί, πότερον χαλεπὸν τοῦ βίου,
ἢ πῶς σὺ αὐτὸ ἐξαγγέλλεις.

329 Ἐγώ σοι, ἔφη, νὴ τὸν Δία ἐρῶ, ὦ Σώκρατες,
οἷόν γέ μοι φαίνεται. πολλάκις γὰρ συνερχόμεθά
τινες εἰς ταὐτὸν παραπλησίαν ἡλικίαν ἔχοντες, διασώ-
ζοντες τὴν παλαιὰν παροιμίαν· οἱ οὖν πλεῖστοι ἡμῶν
5 ὀλοφύρονται συνιόντες, τὰς ἐν τῇ νεότητι ἡδονὰς
ποθοῦντες καὶ ἀναμιμνησκόμενοι περί τε τἀφροδίσια
καὶ περὶ πότους τε καὶ εὐωχίας καὶ ἄλλ' ἄττα ἃ τῶν
τοιούτων ἔχεται, καὶ ἀγανακτοῦσιν ὡς μεγάλων τινῶν
ἀπεστερημένοι καὶ τότε μὲν εὖ ζῶντες, νῦν δὲ οὐδὲ
b ζῶντες. ἔνιοι δὲ καὶ τὰς τῶν οἰκείων προπηλακίσεις
τοῦ γήρως ὀδύρονται, καὶ ἐπὶ τούτῳ δὴ τὸ γῆρας
ὑμνοῦσιν ὅσων κακῶν σφίσιν αἴτιον. ἐμοὶ δὲ δοκοῦσιν,
ὦ Σώκρατες, οὗτοι οὐ τὸ αἴτιον αἰτιᾶσθαι. εἰ γὰρ
5 ἦν τοῦτ' αἴτιον, κἂν ἐγὼ τὰ αὐτὰ ταῦτα ἐπεπόνθη,
ἕνεκά γε γήρως, καὶ οἱ ἄλλοι πάντες ὅσοι ἐνταῦθα

ἦλθον ἡλικίας.] νῦν δ' ἔγωγε ἤδη ἐντετύχηκα οὐχ
οὕτως ἔχουσιν καὶ ἄλλοις, καὶ δὴ καὶ Σοφοκλεῖ ποτε
τῷ ποιητῇ παρεγενόμην ἐρωτωμένῳ ὑπό τινος·
" Πῶς," ἔφη, " ὦ Σοφόκλεις, ἔχεις πρὸς τἀφροδίσια ; c
ἔτι οἷός τε εἶ γυναικὶ συγγίγνεσθαι " ; καὶ ὅς,
" Εὐφήμει," ἔφη, " ὦ ἄνθρωπε· ἀσμενέστατα μέντοι
αὐτὸ ἀπέφυγον, ὥσπερ λυττῶντά τινα καὶ ἄγριον
δεσπότην ἀποφυγών." εὖ οὖν μοι καὶ τότε ἔδοξεν 5
ἐκεῖνος εἰπεῖν, καὶ νῦν οὐχ ἧττον. παντάπασι γὰρ
τῶν γε τοιούτων ἐν τῷ γήρᾳ πολλὴ εἰρήνη γίγνεται
καὶ ἐλευθερία· ἐπειδὰν αἱ ἐπιθυμίαι παύσωνται
κατατείνουσαι καὶ χαλάσωσιν, παντάπασιν τὸ τοῦ
Σοφοκλέους γίγνεται, δεσποτῶν πάνυ πολλῶν ἔστι d
καὶ μαινομένων ἀπηλλάχθαι. ἀλλὰ καὶ τούτων πέρι
καὶ τῶν γε πρὸς τοὺς οἰκείους μία τις αἰτία ἐστίν,
οὐ τὸ γῆρας, ὦ Σώκρατες, ἀλλ' ὁ τρόπος τῶν ἀνθρώπων.
ἂν μὲν γὰρ κόσμιοι καὶ εὔκολοι ὦσιν, καὶ τὸ γῆρας 5
μετρίως ἐστὶν ἐπίπονον· εἰ δὲ μή, καὶ γῆρας, ὦ
Σώκρατες, καὶ νεότης χαλεπὴ τῷ τοιούτῳ συμβαίνει.

Καὶ ἐγὼ ἀγασθεὶς αὐτοῦ εἰπόντος ταῦτα, βουλόμενος ἔτι λέγειν αὐτὸν ἐκίνουν καὶ εἶπον· Ὦ e
Κέφαλε, οἶμαί σου τοὺς πολλούς, ὅταν ταῦτα λέγῃς,
οὐκ ἀποδέχεσθαι ἀλλ' ἡγεῖσθαί σε ῥᾳδίως τὸ γῆρας
φέρειν οὐ διὰ τὸν τρόπον ἀλλὰ διὰ τὸ πολλὴν οὐσίαν
κεκτῆσθαι· τοῖς γὰρ πλουσίοις πολλὰ παραμύθιά 5
φασιν εἶναι.

Ἀληθῆ, ἔφη, λέγεις· οὐ γὰρ ἀποδέχονται. καὶ
λέγουσι μέν τι, οὐ μέντοι γε ὅσον οἴονται· ἀλλὰ τὸ
τοῦ Θεμιστοκλέους εὖ ἔχει, ὃς τῷ Σεριφίῳ λοιδορουμένῳ
καὶ λέγοντι ὅτι οὐ δι' αὑτὸν ἀλλὰ διὰ τὴν πόλιν
εὐδοκιμοῖ, ἀπεκρίνατο ὅτι οὔτ' ἂν αὐτὸς Σερίφιος ὢν 330
ὀνομαστὸς ἐγένετο οὔτ' ἐκεῖνος Ἀθηναῖος. καὶ τοῖς

δὴ μὴ πλουσίοις, χαλεπῶς δὲ τὸ γῆρας φέρουσιν,
εὖ ἔχει ὁ αὐτὸς λόγος, ὅτι οὔτ᾽ ἂν ὁ ἐπιεικὴς πάνυ τι
5 ῥᾳδίως γῆρας μετὰ πενίας ἐνέγκοι οὔθ᾽ ὁ μὴ ἐπιεικὴς
πλουτήσας εὔκολός ποτ᾽ ἂν ἑαυτῷ γένοιτο.

Πότερον δέ, ἦν δ᾽ ἐγώ, ὦ Κέφαλε, ὧν κέκτησαι τὰ
πλείω παρέλαβες ἢ ἐπεκτήσω ;

b Ποῖ᾽ ἐπεκτησάμην, ἔφη, ὦ Σώκρατες ; μέσος τις
γέγονα χρηματιστὴς τοῦ τε πάππου καὶ τοῦ πατρός.
ὁ μὲν γὰρ πάππος τε καὶ ὁμώνυμος ἐμοὶ σχεδόν τι
ὅσην ἐγὼ νῦν οὐσίαν κέκτημαι παραλαβὼν πολλάκις
5 τοσαύτην ἐποίησεν, Λυσανίας δὲ ὁ πατὴρ ἔτι ἐλάττω
αὐτὴν ἐποίησε τῆς νῦν οὔσης· ἐγὼ δὲ ἀγαπῶ ἐὰν μὴ
ἐλάττω καταλίπω τούτοισιν, ἀλλὰ βραχεῖ γέ τινι
πλείω ἢ παρέλαβον.

Οὗ τοι ἕνεκα ἠρόμην, ἦν δ᾽ ἐγώ, ὅτι μοι ἔδοξας οὐ
c σφόδρα ἀγαπᾶν τὰ χρήματα, τοῦτο δὲ ποιοῦσιν ὡς
τὸ πολὺ οἳ ἂν μὴ αὐτοὶ κτήσωνται· οἱ δὲ κτησάμενοι
διπλῇ ἢ οἱ ἄλλοι ἀσπάζονται αὐτά. ὥσπερ γὰρ οἱ
ποιηταὶ τὰ αὑτῶν ποιήματα καὶ οἱ πατέρες τοὺς
5 παῖδας ἀγαπῶσιν, ταύτῃ τε δὴ καὶ οἱ χρηματισάμενοι
περὶ τὰ χρήματα σπουδάζουσιν ὡς ἔργον ἑαυτῶν, καὶ
κατὰ τὴν χρείαν ᾗπερ οἱ ἄλλοι. χαλεποὶ οὖν καὶ
συγγενέσθαι εἰσίν, οὐδὲν ἐθέλοντες ἐπαινεῖν ἀλλ᾽ ἢ τὸν
πλοῦτον.

10 Ἀληθῆ, ἔφη, λέγεις.

d Πάνυ μὲν οὖν, ἦν δ᾽ ἐγώ. ἀλλά μοι ἔτι τοσόνδε
εἰπέ· τί μέγιστον οἴει ἀγαθὸν ἀπολελαυκέναι τοῦ
πολλὴν οὐσίαν κεκτῆσθαι ;

Ὅ, ἦ δ᾽ ὅς, ἴσως οὐκ ἂν πολλοὺς πείσαιμι λέγων.
5 εὖ γὰρ ἴσθι, ἔφη, ὦ Σώκρατες, ὅτι, ἐπειδάν τις ἐγγὺς
ᾖ τοῦ οἴεσθαι τελευτήσειν, εἰσέρχεται αὐτῷ δέος καὶ
φροντὶς περὶ ὧν ἔμπροσθεν οὐκ εἰσῄει. οἵ τε γὰρ

λεγόμενοι μῦθοι περὶ τῶν ἐν Ἅιδου, ὡς τὸν ἐνθάδε
ἀδικήσαντα δεῖ ἐκεῖ διδόναι δίκην, καταγελώμενοι e
τέως, τότε δὴ στρέφουσιν αὐτοῦ τὴν ψυχὴν μὴ
ἀληθεῖς ὦσιν· καὶ αὐτός—ἤτοι ὑπὸ τῆς τοῦ γήρως
ἀσθενείας ἢ καὶ ὥσπερ ἤδη ἐγγυτέρω ὢν τῶν
ἐκεῖ μᾶλλόν τι καθορᾷ αὐτά—ὑποψίας δ᾽ οὖν καὶ 5
δείματος μεστὸς γίγνεται καὶ ἀναλογίζεται ἤδη καὶ
σκοπεῖ εἴ τινά τι ἠδίκηκεν. ὁ μὲν οὖν εὑρίσκων ἑαυτοῦ
ἐν τῷ βίῳ πολλὰ ἀδικήματα καὶ ἐκ τῶν ὕπνων,
ὥσπερ οἱ παῖδες, θαμὰ ἐγειρόμενος δειμαίνει καὶ ζῇ
μετὰ κακῆς ἐλπίδος· τῷ δὲ μηδὲν ἑαυτῷ ἄδικον 331
συνειδότι ἡδεῖα ἐλπὶς ἀεὶ πάρεστι καὶ ἀγαθὴ γηροτ-
ρόφος, ὡς καὶ Πίνδαρος λέγει. χαριέντως γάρ τοι,
ὦ Σώκρατες, τοῦτ᾽ ἐκεῖνος εἶπεν, ὅτι ὃς ἂν δικαίως
καὶ ὁσίως τὸν βίον διαγάγῃ,   5

> γλυκεῖά οἱ καρδίαν
> ἀτάλλοισα γηροτρόφος συναορεῖ
> ἐλπὶς ἃ μάλιστα θνατῶν πολύστροφον
> γνώμαν κυβερνᾷ.

εὖ οὖν λέγει θαυμαστῶς ὡς σφόδρα. πρὸς δὴ τοῦτ᾽ 10
ἔγωγε τίθημι τὴν τῶν χρημάτων κτῆσιν πλείστου
ἀξίαν εἶναι, οὔ τι παντὶ ἀνδρὶ ἀλλὰ τῷ ἐπιεικεῖ καὶ b
κοσμίῳ. τὸ γὰρ μηδὲ ἄκοντά τινα ἐξαπατῆσαι ἢ
ψεύσασθαι, μηδ᾽ αὖ ὀφείλοντα ἢ θεῷ θυσίας τινὰς
ἢ ἀνθρώπῳ χρήματα ἔπειτα ἐκεῖσε ἀπιέναι δεδιότα,
μέγα μέρος εἰς τοῦτο ἡ τῶν χρημάτων κτῆσις 5
συμβάλλεται. ἔχει δὲ καὶ ἄλλας χρείας πολλάς·
ἀλλά γε ἓν ἀνθ᾽ ἑνὸς οὐκ ἐλάχιστον ἔγωγε θείην
ἂν εἰς τοῦτο ἀνδρὶ νοῦν ἔχοντι, ὦ Σώκρατες, πλοῦτον
χρησιμώτατον εἶναι.

Παγκάλως, ἦν δ᾽ ἐγώ, λέγεις, ὦ Κέφαλε. τοῦτο δ᾽ c
αὐτό, τὴν δικαιοσύνην, πότερα τὴν ἀλήθειαν αὐτὸ

φήσομεν εἶναι ἁπλῶς οὕτως καὶ τὸ ἀποδιδόναι ἄν
τίς τι παρά του λάβῃ, ἢ καὶ αὐτὰ ταῦτα ἔστιν ἐνίοτε
5 μὲν δικαίως, ἐνίοτε δὲ ἀδίκως ποιεῖν ; οἷον τοιόνδε
λέγω· πᾶς ἄν που εἴποι, εἴ τις λάβοι παρὰ φίλου
ἀνδρὸς σωφρονοῦντος ὅπλα, εἰ μανεὶς ἀπαιτοῖ, ὅτι
οὔτε χρὴ τὰ τοιαῦτα ἀποδιδόναι, οὔτε δίκαιος ἂν εἴη ὁ
ἀποδιδούς, οὐδ' αὖ πρὸς τὸν οὕτως ἔχοντα πάντα
10 ἐθέλων τἀληθῆ λέγειν.

d Ὀρθῶς, ἔφη, λέγεις.

Οὐκ ἄρα οὗτος ὅρος ἐστὶν δικαιοσύνης, ἀληθῆ τε
λέγειν καὶ ἃ ἂν λάβῃ τις ἀποδιδόναι.

Πάνυ μὲν οὖν, ἔφη, ὦ Σώκρατες, ὑπολαβὼν ὁ
5 Πολέμαρχος, εἴπερ γέ τι χρὴ Σιμωνίδῃ πείθεσθαι.

Καὶ μέντοι, ἔφη ὁ Κέφαλος, καὶ παραδίδωμι ὑμῖν
τὸν λόγον· δεῖ γάρ με ἤδη τῶν ἱερῶν ἐπιμεληθῆναι.

Οὐκοῦν, ἔφη, ἐγώ, ὁ Πολέμαρχος, τῶν γε σῶν
κληρονόμος ;

10 Πάνυ γε, ἦ δ' ὃς γελάσας, καὶ ἅμα ᾔει πρὸς τὰ
ἱερά.

e Λέγε δή, εἶπον ἐγώ, σὺ ὁ τοῦ λόγου κληρονόμος,
τί φῂς τὸν Σιμωνίδην λέγοντα ὀρθῶς λέγειν περὶ
δικαιοσύνης ;

Ὅτι, ἦ δ' ὅς, τὸ τὰ ὀφειλόμενα ἑκάστῳ ἀποδιδόναι
5 δίκαιόν ἐστι· τοῦτο λέγων δοκεῖ ἔμοιγε καλῶς λέγειν.

Ἀλλὰ μέντοι, ἦν δ' ἐγώ, Σιμωνίδῃ γε οὐ ῥᾴδιον
ἀπιστεῖν· σοφὸς γὰρ καὶ θεῖος ἀνήρ· τοῦτο μέντοι ὅτι
ποτὲ λέγει, σὺ μέν, ὦ Πολέμαρχε, ἴσως γιγνώσκεις,
ἐγὼ δὲ ἀγνοῶ· δῆλον γὰρ ὅτι οὐ τοῦτο λέγει, ὅπερ
10 ἄρτι ἐλέγομεν, τό τινος παρακαταθεμένου τι ὁτῳοῦν
332 μὴ σωφρόνως ἀπαιτοῦντι ἀποδιδόναι. καίτοι γε ὀφει-
λόμενόν πού ἐστι τοῦτο ὃ παρακατέθετο· ἦ γάρ ;

Ναί.

Ἀποδοτέον δέ γε οὐδ' ὁπωστιοῦν τότε ὁπότε τις
μὴ σωφρόνως ἀπαιτοῖ ;   5
Ἀληθῆ, ἦ δ' ὅς.
Ἄλλο δή τι ἢ τὸ τοιοῦτον, ὡς ἔοικεν, λέγει Σιμωνίδης
τὸ τὰ ὀφειλόμενα δίκαιον εἶναι ἀποδιδόναι.
Ἄλλο μέντοι νὴ Δί', ἔφη· τοῖς γὰρ φίλοις οἴεται
ὀφείλειν τοὺς φίλους ἀγαθὸν μέν τι δρᾶν, κακὸν δὲ 10
μηδέν.
Μανθάνω, ἦν δ' ἐγώ—ὅτι οὐ τὰ ὀφειλόμενα ἀπο-
δίδωσιν ὃς ἄν τῳ χρυσίον ἀποδῷ παρακαταθεμένῳ,
ἐάνπερ ἡ ἀπόδοσις καὶ ἡ λῆψις βλαβερὰ γίγνηται, b
φίλοι δὲ ὦσιν ὅ τε ἀπολαμβάνων καὶ ὁ ἀποδιδούς—
οὐχ οὕτω λέγειν φῂς τὸν Σιμωνίδην ;
Πάνυ μὲν οὖν.
Τί δέ ; τοῖς ἐχθροῖς ἀποδοτέον ὅτι ἂν τύχῃ ὀφει- 5
λόμενον ;
Παντάπασι μὲν οὖν, ἔφη, ὅ γε ὀφείλεται αὐτοῖς, ὀφείλεται δέ γε οἶμαι παρά γε τοῦ ἐχθροῦ τῷ ἐχθρῷ ὅπερ
καὶ προσήκει, κακόν τι.
Ἠινίξατο ἄρα, ἦν δ' ἐγώ, ὡς ἔοικεν, ὁ Σιμωνίδης 10
ποιητικῶς τὸ δίκαιον ὃ εἴη. διενοεῖτο μὲν γάρ, ὡς c
φαίνεται, ὅτι τοῦτ' εἴη δίκαιον, τὸ προσῆκον ἑκάστῳ
ἀποδιδόναι, τοῦτο δὲ ὠνόμασεν ὀφειλόμενον.
Ἀλλὰ τί οἴει ; ἔφη.
Ὦ πρὸς Διός, ἦν δ' ἐγώ, εἰ οὖν τις αὐτὸν ἤρετο· 5
" Ὦ Σιμωνίδη, ἡ τίσιν οὖν τί ἀποδιδοῦσα ὀφειλόμενον
καὶ προσῆκον τέχνη ἰατρικὴ καλεῖται ; " τί ἂν οἴει
ἡμῖν αὐτὸν ἀποκρίνασθαι ;
Δῆλον ὅτι, ἔφη, ἡ σώμασιν φάρμακά τε καὶ σιτία
καὶ ποτά.   10
Ἡ δὲ τίσιν τί ἀποδιδοῦσα ὀφειλόμενον καὶ προσῆκον
τέχνη μαγειρικὴ καλεῖται ;

d　'Η τοῖς ὄψοις τὰ ἡδύσματα.

Εἶεν· ἡ οὖν δὴ τίσιν τί ἀποδιδοῦσα τέχνη δικαιοσύνη
ἂν καλοῖτο ;

Εἰ μέν τι, ἔφη, δεῖ ἀκολουθεῖν, ὦ Σώκρατες, τοῖς
5 ἔμπροσθεν εἰρημένοις, ἡ τοῖς φίλοις τε καὶ ἐχθροῖς
ὠφελίας τε καὶ βλάβας ἀποδιδοῦσα.

Τὸ τοὺς φίλους ἄρα εὖ ποιεῖν καὶ τοὺς ἐχθροὺς
κακῶς δικαιοσύνην λέγει ;

Δοκεῖ μοι.

10　Τίς οὖν δυνατώτατος κάμνοντας φίλους εὖ ποιεῖν καὶ
ἐχθροὺς κακῶς πρὸς νόσον καὶ ὑγίειαν ;

Ἰατρός.

e　Τίς δὲ πλέοντας πρὸς τὸν τῆς θαλάττης κίνδυνον ;

Κυβερνήτης.

Τί δὲ ὁ δίκαιος ; ἐν τίνι πράξει καὶ πρὸς τί ἔργον
δυνατώτατος φίλους ὠφελεῖν καὶ ἐχθροὺς βλάπτειν ;

5　Ἐν τῷ προσπολεμεῖν καὶ ἐν τῷ συμμαχεῖν, ἔμοιγε
δοκεῖ.

Εἶεν· μὴ κάμνουσί γε μήν, ὦ φίλε Πολέμαρχε,
ἰατρὸς ἄχρηστος.

Ἀληθῆ.

10　Καὶ μὴ πλέουσι δὴ κυβερνήτης.

Ναί.

Ἆρα καὶ τοῖς μὴ πολεμοῦσιν ὁ δίκαιος ἄχρηστος ;

Οὐ πάνυ μοι δοκεῖ τοῦτο.

Χρήσιμον ἄρα καὶ ἐν εἰρήνῃ δικαιοσύνη ;

333　Χρήσιμον.

Καὶ γὰρ γεωργία· ἢ οὔ ;

Ναί.

Πρός γε καρποῦ κτῆσιν ;

5　Ναί.

Καὶ μὴν καὶ σκυτοτομική ;

Ναί.

Πρός γε ὑποδημάτων ἂν οἶμαι φαίης κτῆσιν ;

Πάνυ γε.

Τί δὲ δή ; τὴν δικαιοσύνην πρὸς τίνος χρείαν ἢ 10
κτῆσιν ἐν εἰρήνῃ φαίης ἂν χρήσιμον εἶναι ;

Πρὸς τὰ συμβόλαια, ὦ Σώκρατες.

Συμβόλαια δὲ λέγεις κοινωνήματα ἤ τι ἄλλο ;

Κοινωνήματα δῆτα.

· Ἆρ' οὖν ὁ δίκαιος ἀγαθὸς καὶ χρήσιμος κοινωνὸς **b**
εἰς πεττῶν θέσιν, ἢ ὁ πεττευτικός ;

Ὁ πεττευτικός.

Ἀλλ' εἰς πλίνθων καὶ λίθων θέσιν ὁ δίκαιος χρησιμ-
ώτερός τε καὶ ἀμείνων κοινωνὸς τοῦ οἰκοδομικοῦ ; **5**

Οὐδαμῶς.

Ἀλλ' εἰς τίνα δὴ κοινωνίαν ὁ δίκαιος ἀμείνων
κοινωνὸς τοῦ κιθαριστικοῦ, ὥσπερ ὁ κιθαριστικὸς τοῦ
δικαίου εἰς κρουμάτων ;

Εἰς ἀργυρίου, ἔμοιγε δοκεῖ. **10**

Πλήν γ' ἴσως, ὦ Πολέμαρχε, πρὸς τὸ χρῆσθαι
ἀργυρίῳ, ὅταν δέῃ ἀργυρίου κοινῇ πρίασθαι ἢ ἀποδόσθαι
ἵππον· τότε δέ, ὡς ἐγὼ οἶμαι, ὁ ἱππικός. ἢ γάρ ; **c**

Φαίνεται.

Καὶ μὴν ὅταν γε πλοῖον, ὁ ναυπηγὸς ἢ ὁ κυβερνήτης ;

Ἔοικεν.

Ὅταν οὖν τί δέῃ ἀργυρίῳ ἢ χρυσίῳ κοινῇ χρῆσθαι, **5**
ὁ δίκαιος χρησιμώτερος τῶν ἄλλων ;

Ὅταν παρακαταθέσθαι καὶ σῶν εἶναι, ὦ Σώκρατες.

Οὐκοῦν λέγεις ὅταν μηδὲν δέῃ αὐτῷ χρῆσθαι ἀλλὰ
κεῖσθαι ;

Πάνυ γε. **10**

Ὅταν ἄρα ἄχρηστον ᾖ ἀργύριον, τότε χρήσιμος
ἐπ' αὐτῷ ἡ δικαιοσύνη ; **d**

Κινδυνεύει.

Καὶ ὅταν δὴ δρέπανον δέῃ φυλάττειν, ἡ δικαιοσύνη
χρήσιμος καὶ κοινῇ καὶ ἰδίᾳ· ὅταν δὲ χρῆσθαι, ἡ
5 ἀμπελουργική ;

Φαίνεται.

Φήσεις δὲ καὶ ἀσπίδα καὶ λύραν ὅταν δέῃ φυλάττειν
καὶ μηδὲν χρῆσθαι, χρήσιμον εἶναι τὴν δικαιοσύνην,
ὅταν δὲ χρῆσθαι, τὴν ὁπλιτικὴν καὶ τὴν μουσικήν ;

10 Ἀνάγκη.

Καὶ περὶ τἆλλα δὴ πάντα ἡ δικαιοσύνη ἑκάστου
ἐν μὲν χρήσει ἄχρηστος, ἐν δὲ ἀχρηστίᾳ χρήσιμος ;

Κινδυνεύει.

θ Οὐκ ἂν οὖν, ὦ φίλε, πάνυ γέ τι σπουδαῖον εἴη ἡ
δικαιοσύνη, εἰ πρὸς τὰ ἄχρηστα χρήσιμον ὂν τυγχάνει.
τόδε δὲ σκεψώμεθα. ἆρ' οὐχ ὁ πατάξαι δεινότατος
ἐν μάχῃ εἴτε πυκτικῇ εἴτε τινὶ καὶ ἄλλῃ, οὗτος καὶ
5 φυλάξασθαι ;

Πάνυ γε.

Ἆρ' οὖν καὶ νόσον ὅστις δεινὸς φυλάξασθαι, καὶ
λαθεῖν οὗτος δεινότατος ἐμποιήσας ;

Ἔμοιγε δοκεῖ.

334 Ἀλλὰ μὴν στρατοπέδου γε ὁ αὐτὸς φύλαξ ἀγαθός,
ὅσπερ καὶ τὰ τῶν πολεμίων κλέψαι καὶ βουλεύματα
καὶ τὰς ἄλλας πράξεις ;

Πάνυ γε.

5 Ὅτου τις ἄρα δεινὸς φύλαξ, τούτου καὶ φὼρ δεινός.

Ἔοικεν.

Εἰ ἄρα ὁ δίκαιος ἀργύριον δεινὸς φυλάττειν, καὶ
κλέπτειν δεινός.

Ὡς γοῦν ὁ λόγος, ἔφη, σημαίνει.

10 Κλέπτης ἄρα τις ὁ δίκαιος, ὡς ἔοικεν, ἀναπέφανται,
καὶ κινδυνεύεις παρ' Ὁμήρου μεμαθηκέναι αὐτό· καὶ

γὰρ ἐκεῖνος τὸν τοῦ Ὀδυσσέως πρὸς μητρὸς πάππον **b**
Αὐτόλυκον ἀγαπᾷ τε καὶ φησιν αὐτὸν πάντας ἀνθρώπους
κεκάσθαι κλεπτοσύνῃ θ᾽ ὅρκῳ τε. ἔοικεν οὖν ἡ
δικαιοσύνη καὶ κατὰ σὲ καὶ καθ᾽ Ὅμηρον καὶ κατὰ
Σιμωνίδην κλεπτική τις εἶναι, ἐπ᾽ ὠφελίᾳ μέντοι τῶν 5
φίλων καὶ ἐπὶ βλάβῃ τῶν ἐχθρῶν. οὐχ οὕτως ἔλεγες ;

Οὐ μὰ τὸν Δί᾽, ἔφη, ἀλλ᾽ οὐκέτι οἶδα ἔγωγε ὅτι
ἔλεγον· τοῦτο μέντοι ἔμοιγε δοκεῖ ἔτι, ὠφελεῖν μὲν
τοὺς φίλους ἡ δικαιοσύνη, βλάπτειν δὲ τοὺς ἐχθρούς.

Φίλους δὲ λέγεις εἶναι πότερον τοὺς δοκοῦντας **c**
ἑκάστῳ χρηστοὺς εἶναι, ἢ τοὺς ὄντας, κἂν μὴ δοκῶσι,
καὶ ἐχθροὺς ὡσαύτως ;

Εἰκὸς μέν, ἔφη, οὓς ἄν τις ἡγῆται χρηστοὺς φιλεῖν,
οὓς δ᾽ ἂν πονηροὺς μισεῖν.   5

Ἆρ᾽ οὖν οὐχ ἁμαρτάνουσιν οἱ ἄνθρωποι περὶ
τοῦτο, ὥστε δοκεῖν αὐτοῖς πολλοὺς μὲν χρηστοὺς εἶναι
μὴ ὄντας, πολλοὺς δὲ τοὐναντίον ;

Ἁμαρτάνουσιν.

Τούτοις ἄρα οἱ μὲν ἀγαθοὶ ἐχθροί, οἱ δὲ κακοὶ **10**
φίλοι ;

Πάνυ γε.

Ἀλλ᾽ ὅμως δίκαιον τότε τούτοις τοὺς μὲν πονηροὺς
ὠφελεῖν, τοὺς δὲ ἀγαθοὺς βλάπτειν ;   **d**

Φαίνεται.

Ἀλλὰ μὴν οἵ γε ἀγαθοὶ δίκαιοί τε καὶ οἷοι μὴ
ἀδικεῖν ;

Ἀληθῆ.   5

Κατὰ δὴ τὸν σὸν λόγον τοὺς μηδὲν ἀδικοῦντας
δίκαιον κακῶς ποιεῖν.

Μηδαμῶς, ἔφη, ὦ Σώκρατες· πονηρὸς γὰρ ἔοικεν
εἶναι ὁ λόγος.

Τοὺς ἀδίκους ἄρα, ἦν δ᾽ ἐγώ, δίκαιον βλάπτειν, **10**

τοὺς δὲ δικαίους ὠφελεῖν ;

Οὗτος ἐκείνου καλλίων φαίνεται.

Πολλοῖς ἄρα, ὦ Πολέμαρχε, συμβήσεται, ὅσοι διημαρτήκασιν τῶν ἀνθρώπων, δίκαιον εἶναι τοὺς μὲν e φίλους βλάπτειν· πονηροὶ γὰρ αὐτοῖς εἰσιν· τοὺς δ' ἐχθροὺς ὠφελεῖν· ἀγαθοὶ γάρ· καὶ οὕτως ἐροῦμεν αὐτὸ τοὐναντίον ἢ τὸν Σιμωνίδην ἔφαμεν λέγειν.

Καὶ μάλα, ἔφη, οὕτω συμβαίνει. ἀλλὰ μεταθώμεθα· 5 κινδυνεύομεν γὰρ οὐκ ὀρθῶς τὸν φίλον καὶ ἐχθρὸν θέσθαι.

Πῶς θέμενοι, ὦ Πολέμαρχε ;

Τὸν δοκοῦντα χρηστόν, τοῦτον φίλον εἶναι.

Νῦν δὲ πῶς, ἦν δ' ἐγώ, μεταθώμεθα ;

10 Τὸν δοκοῦντά τε, ἦ δ' ὅς, καὶ τὸν ὄντα χρηστὸν 335 φίλον· τὸν δὲ δοκοῦντα μέν, ὄντα δὲ μή, δοκεῖν ἀλλὰ μὴ εἶναι φίλον. καὶ περὶ τοῦ ἐχθροῦ δὲ ἡ αὐτὴ θέσις.

Φίλος μὲν δή, ὡς ἔοικε, τούτῳ τῷ λόγῳ ὁ ἀγαθὸς ἔσται, ἐχθρὸς δὲ ὁ πονηρός.

5 Ναί.

Κελεύεις δὴ ἡμᾶς προσθεῖναι τῷ δικαίῳ [ἢ] ὡς τὸ πρῶτον ἐλέγομεν, λέγοντες δίκαιον εἶναι τὸν μὲν φίλον εὖ ποιεῖν, τὸν δ' ἐχθρὸν κακῶς· νῦν πρὸς τούτῳ ὧδε λέγειν, ὅτι ἔστιν δίκαιον τὸν μὲν φίλον 10 ἀγαθὸν ὄντα εὖ ποιεῖν, τὸν δ' ἐχθρὸν κακὸν ὄντα βλάπτειν ;

b Πάνυ μὲν οὖν, ἔφη, οὕτως ἄν μοι δοκεῖ καλῶς λέγεσθαι.

Ἔστιν ἄρα, ἦν δ' ἐγώ, δικαίου ἀνδρὸς βλάπτειν καὶ ὁντινοῦν ἀνθρώπων ;

5 Καὶ πάνυ γε, ἔφη· τούς γε πονηρούς τε καὶ ἐχθροὺς δεῖ βλάπτειν.

Βλαπτόμενοι δ' ἵπποι βελτίους ἢ χείρους γίγνονται ;

Χείρους.

Ἆρα εἰς τὴν τῶν κυνῶν ἀρετήν, ἢ εἰς τὴν τῶν
ἵππων ;   10

Εἰς τὴν τῶν ἵππων.

Ἆρ' οὖν καὶ κύνες βλαπτόμενοι χείρους γίγνονται
εἰς τὴν τῶν κυνῶν ἀλλ' οὐκ εἰς τὴν τῶν ἵππων ἀρετήν ;

Ἀνάγκη.

Ἀνθρώπους δέ, ὦ ἑταῖρε, μὴ οὕτω φῶμεν, βλαπτο- c
μένους εἰς τὴν ἀνθρωπείαν ἀρετὴν χείρους γίγνεσθαι ;

Πάνυ μὲν οὖν.

Ἀλλ' ἡ δικαιοσύνη οὐκ ἀνθρωπεία ἀρετή ;

Καὶ τοῦτ' ἀνάγκη.   5

Καὶ τοὺς βλαπτομένους ἄρα, ὦ φίλε, τῶν ἀνθρώπων
ἀνάγκη ἀδικωτέρους γίγνεσθαι.

Ἔοικεν.

Ἆρ' οὖν τῇ μουσικῇ οἱ μουσικοὶ ἀμούσους δύνανται
ποιεῖν ;   10

Ἀδύνατον.

Ἀλλὰ τῇ ἱππικῇ οἱ ἱππικοὶ ἀφίππους ;

Οὐκ ἔστιν.

Ἀλλὰ τῇ δικαιοσύνῃ δὴ οἱ δίκαιοι ἀδίκους ;   ἢ
καὶ συλλήβδην ἀρετῇ οἱ ἀγαθοὶ κακούς ;   d

Ἀλλὰ ἀδύνατον.

Οὐ γὰρ θερμότητος οἶμαι ἔργον ψύχειν ἀλλὰ τοῦ
ἐναντίου.

Ναί.   5

Οὐδὲ ξηρότητος ὑγραίνειν ἀλλὰ τοῦ ἐναντίου.

Πάνυ γε.

Οὐδὲ δὴ τοῦ ἀγαθοῦ βλάπτειν ἀλλὰ τοῦ ἐναντίου.

Φαίνεται.

Ὁ δέ γε δίκαιος ἀγαθός ;   10

Πάνυ γε.

Οὐκ ἄρα τοῦ δικαίου βλάπτειν ἔργον, ὦ Πολέμαρχε,
οὔτε φίλον οὔτ᾽ ἄλλον οὐδένα, ἀλλὰ τοῦ ἐναντίου, τοῦ
ἀδίκου.

15 Παντάπασί μοι δοκεῖς ἀληθῆ λέγειν, ἔφη, ὦ
Σώκρατες.

θ Εἰ ἄρα τὰ ὀφειλόμενα ἑκάστῳ ἀποδιδόναι φησίν
τις δίκαιον εἶναι, τοῦτο δὲ δὴ νοεῖ αὐτῷ τοῖς μὲν
ἐχθροῖς βλάβην ὀφείλεσθαι παρὰ τοῦ δικαίου ἀνδρός,
τοῖς δὲ φίλοις ὠφελίαν, οὐκ ἦν σοφὸς ὁ ταῦτα εἰπών.
5 οὐ γὰρ ἀληθῆ ἔλεγεν· οὐδαμοῦ γὰρ δίκαιον οὐδένα
ἡμῖν ἐφάνη ὂν βλάπτειν.

Συγχωρῶ, ἦ δ᾽ ὅς.

Μαχούμεθα ἄρα, ἦν δ᾽ ἐγώ, κοινῇ ἐγώ τε καὶ σύ, ἐάν
τις αὐτὸ φῇ ἢ Σιμωνίδην ἢ Βίαντα ἢ Πιττακὸν εἰρη-
10 κέναι ἤ τιν᾽ ἄλλον τῶν σοφῶν τε καὶ μακαρίων ἀνδρῶν.

Ἐγὼ γοῦν, ἔφη, ἕτοιμός εἰμι κοινωνεῖν τῆς μάχης.

336 Ἀλλ᾽ οἶσθα, ἦν δ᾽ ἐγώ, οὗ μοι δοκεῖ εἶναι τὸ ῥῆμα,
τὸ φάναι δίκαιον εἶναι τοὺς μὲν φίλους ὠφελεῖν, τοὺς
δ᾽ ἐχθροὺς βλάπτειν;

Τίνος; ἔφη.

5 Οἶμαι αὐτὸ Περιάνδρου εἶναι ἢ Περδίκκου ἢ
Ξέρξου ἢ Ἰσμηνίου τοῦ Θηβαίου ἤ τινος ἄλλου μέγα
οἰομένου δύνασθαι πλουσίου ἀνδρός.

Ἀληθέστατα, ἔφη, λέγεις.

Εἶεν, ἦν δ᾽ ἐγώ· ἐπειδὴ δὲ οὐδὲ τοῦτο ἐφάνη ἡ
10 δικαιοσύνη ὂν οὐδὲ τὸ δίκαιον, τί ἂν ἄλλο τις αὐτὸ
φαίη εἶναι;

b Καὶ ὁ Θρασύμαχος πολλάκις μὲν καὶ διαλεγομένων
ἡμῶν μεταξὺ ὥρμα ἀντιλαμβάνεσθαι τοῦ λόγου,
ἔπειτα ὑπὸ τῶν παρακαθημένων διεκωλύετο βουλο-
μένων διακοῦσαι τὸν λόγον· ὡς δὲ διεπαυσάμεθα καὶ
5 ἐγὼ ταῦτ᾽ εἶπον, οὐκέτι ἡσυχίαν ἦγεν, ἀλλὰ συστρέψας

ἑαυτὸν ὥσπερ θηρίον ἧκεν ἐφ᾽ ἡμᾶς ὡς διαρπασό-
μενος.

Καὶ ἐγώ τε καὶ ὁ Πολέμαρχος δείσαντες διεπτοή-
θημεν· ὁ δ᾽ εἰς τὸ μέσον φθεγξάμενος, Τίς, ἔφη, ὑμᾶς
πάλαι φλυαρία ἔχει, ὦ Σώκρατες ; καὶ τί εὐηθίζεσθε c
πρὸς ἀλλήλους ὑποκατακλινόμενοι ὑμῖν αὐτοῖς ; ἀλλ᾽
εἴπερ ὡς ἀληθῶς βούλει εἰδέναι τὸ δίκαιον ὅτι ἔστι, μὴ
μόνον ἐρώτα μηδὲ φιλοτιμοῦ ἐλέγχων ἐπειδάν τίς τι
ἀποκρίνηται, ἐγνωκὼς τοῦτο, ὅτι ῥᾷον ἐρωτᾶν ἢ 5
ἀποκρίνεσθαι, ἀλλὰ καὶ αὐτὸς ἀπόκριναι καὶ εἰπὲ τί
φῂς εἶναι τὸ δίκαιον. καὶ ὅπως μοι μὴ ἐρεῖς ὅτι τὸ
δέον ἐστὶν μηδ᾽ ὅτι τὸ ὠφέλιμον μηδ᾽ ὅτι τὸ λυσιτελοῦν d
μηδ᾽ ὅτι τὸ κερδαλέον μηδ᾽ ὅτι τὸ συμφέρον, ἀλλὰ
σαφῶς μοι καὶ ἀκριβῶς λέγε ὅτι ἂν λέγῃς· ὡς ἐγὼ
οὐκ ἀποδέξομαι ἐὰν ὕθλους τοιούτους λέγῃς.

Καὶ ἐγὼ ἀκούσας ἐξεπλάγην καὶ προσβλέπων 5
αὐτὸν ἐφοβούμην, καί μοι δοκῶ, εἰ μὴ πρότερος ἑωράκη
αὐτὸν ἢ ἐκεῖνος ἐμέ, ἄφωνος ἂν γενέσθαι. νῦν δὲ
ἡνίκα ὑπὸ τοῦ λόγου ἤρχετο ἐξαγριαίνεσθαι, προσέ-
βλεψα αὐτὸν πρότερος, ὥστε αὐτῷ οἷός τ᾽ ἐγενόμην e
ἀποκρίνασθαι, καὶ εἶπον ὑποτρέμων· Ὦ Θρασύμαχε,
μὴ χαλεπὸς ἡμῖν ἴσθι· εἰ γάρ τι ἐξαμαρτάνομεν ἐν
τῇ τῶν λόγων σκέψει ἐγώ τε καὶ ὅδε, εὖ ἴσθι ὅτι
ἄκοντες ἁμαρτάνομεν. μὴ γὰρ δὴ οἴου, εἰ μὲν χρυσίον 5
ἐζητοῦμεν, οὐκ ἄν ποτε ἡμᾶς ἑκόντας εἶναι ὑποκατακλίνεσθαι ἀλλήλοις ἐν τῇ ζητήσει καὶ διαφθείρειν τὴν
εὕρεσιν αὐτοῦ, δικαιοσύνην δὲ ζητοῦντας, πρᾶγμα
πολλῶν χρυσίων τιμιώτερον, ἔπειθ᾽ οὕτως ἀνοήτως
ὑπείκειν ἀλλήλοις καὶ οὐ σπουδάζειν ὅτι μάλιστα 10
φανῆναι αὐτό. οἴου γε σύ, ὦ φίλε. ἀλλ᾽ οἶμαι οὐ
δυνάμεθα· ἐλεεῖσθαι οὖν ἡμᾶς πολὺ μᾶλλον εἰκός 337
ἐστίν που ὑπὸ ὑμῶν τῶν δεινῶν ἢ χαλεπαίνεσθαι.

Καὶ ὃς ἀκούσας ἀνεκάγχασέ τε μάλα σαρδάνιον καὶ
εἶπεν· Ὦ Ἡράκλεις, ἔφη, αὕτη 'κείνη ἡ εἰωθυῖα
5 εἰρωνεία Σωκράτους, καὶ ταῦτ' ἐγὼ ᾔδη τε καὶ
τούτοις προύλεγον, ὅτι σὺ ἀποκρίνασθαι μὲν οὐκ
ἐθελήσοις, εἰρωνεύσοιο δὲ καὶ πάντα μᾶλλον ποιήσοις
ἢ ἀποκρινοῖο, εἴ τίς τί σε ἐρωτᾷ.

Σοφὸς γὰρ εἶ, ἦν δ' ἐγώ, ὦ Θρασύμαχε· εὖ οὖν
10 ᾔδησθα ὅτι εἴ τινα ἔροιο ὁπόσα ἐστὶν τὰ δώδεκα, καὶ
b ἐρόμενος προείποις αὐτῷ—" Ὅπως μοι, ὦ ἄνθρωπε,
μὴ ἐρεῖς ὅτι, ἔστιν τὰ δώδεκα δὶς ἓξ μηδ' ὅτι τρὶς
τέτταρα μηδ' ὅτι ἑξάκις δύο μηδ' ὅτι τετράκις τρία·
ὡς οὐκ ἀποδέξομαί σου ἐὰν τοιαῦτα φλυαρῇς "—
5 δῆλον οἶμαί σοι ἦν ὅτι οὐδεὶς ἀποκρινοῖτο τῷ
οὕτως πυνθανομένῳ. ἀλλ' εἴ σοι εἶπεν· " Ὦ
Θρασύμαχε, πῶς λέγεις; μὴ ἀποκρίνωμαι ὧν
προεῖπες μηδέν; πότερον, ὦ θαυμάσιε, μηδ'
εἰ τούτων τι τυγχάνει ὄν, ἀλλ' ἕτερον εἴπω τι τοῦ
c ἀληθοῦς; ἢ πῶς λέγεις "; τί ἂν αὐτῷ εἶπες πρὸς
ταῦτα;

Εἶεν, ἔφη· ὡς δὴ ὅμοιον τοῦτο ἐκείνῳ.

Οὐδέν γε κωλύει, ἦν δ' ἐγώ· εἰ δ' οὖν καὶ μὴ ἔστιν
5 ὅμοιον, φαίνεται δὲ τῷ ἐρωτηθέντι τοιοῦτον, ἧττόν
τι αὐτὸν οἴει ἀποκρινεῖσθαι τὸ φαινόμενον ἑαυτῷ,
ἐάντε ἡμεῖς ἀπαγορεύωμεν ἐάντε μή;

Ἄλλο τι οὖν, ἔφη, καὶ σὺ οὕτω ποιήσεις· ὧν ἐγὼ
ἀπεῖπον, τούτων τι ἀποκρινῇ;

10 Οὐκ ἂν θαυμάσαιμι, ἦν δ' ἐγώ· εἴ μοι σκεψαμένῳ
οὕτω δόξειεν.

d Τί οὖν, ἔφη, ἂν ἐγὼ δείξω ἑτέραν ἀπόκρισιν παρὰ
πάσας ταύτας περὶ δικαιοσύνης, βελτίω τούτων; τί
ἀξιοῖς παθεῖν;

Τί ἄλλο, ἦν δ' ἐγώ, ἢ ὅπερ προσήκει πάσχειν τῷ

μὴ εἰδότι ; προσήκει δέ που μαθεῖν παρὰ τοῦ εἰδότος· 5
καὶ ἐγὼ οὖν τοῦτο ἀξιῶ παθεῖν.

Ἡδὺς γὰρ εἶ, ἔφη· ἀλλὰ πρὸς τῷ μαθεῖν καὶ
ἀπότεισον ἀργύριον.

Οὐκοῦν ἐπειδάν μοι γένηται, εἶπον.

Ἀλλ' ἔστιν, ἔφη ὁ Γλαύκων. ἀλλ' ἕνεκα ἀργυρίου, 10
ὦ Θρασύμαχε, λέγε· πάντες γὰρ ἡμεῖς Σωκράτει
εἰσοίσομεν.

Πάνυ γε οἶμαι, ἦ δ' ὅς· ἵνα Σωκράτης τὸ εἰωθὸς e
διαπράξηται· αὐτὸς μὲν μὴ ἀποκρίνηται, ἄλλου δ'
ἀποκρινομένου λαμβάνῃ λόγον καὶ ἐλέγχῃ.

Πῶς γὰρ ἄν, ἔφην ἐγώ, ὦ βέλτιστε, τὶς ἀποκρίναιτο
πρῶτον μὲν μὴ εἰδὼς μηδὲ φάσκων εἰδέναι, ἔπειτα, 5
εἴ τι καὶ οἴεται, περὶ τούτων ἀπειρημένον αὐτῷ εἴη
ὅπως μηδὲν ἐρεῖ ὧν ἡγεῖται ὑπ' ἀνδρὸς οὐ φαύλου ;
ἀλλὰ σὲ δὴ μᾶλλον εἰκὸς λέγειν· σὺ γὰρ δὴ φὴς 338
εἰδέναι καὶ ἔχειν εἰπεῖν. μὴ οὖν ἄλλως ποίει, ἀλλὰ
ἐμοί τε χαρίζου ἀποκρινόμενος καὶ μὴ φθονήσῃς καὶ
Γλαύκωνα τόνδε διδάξαι καὶ τοὺς ἄλλους.

Εἰπόντος δέ μου ταῦτα, ὅ τε Γλαύκων καὶ οἱ ἄλλοι 5
ἐδέοντο αὐτοῦ μὴ ἄλλως ποιεῖν. καὶ ὁ Θρασύμαχος
φανερὸς μὲν ἦν ἐπιθυμῶν εἰπεῖν ἵν' εὐδοκιμήσειεν,
ἡγούμενος ἔχειν ἀπόκρισιν παγκάλην· προσεποιεῖτο
δὲ φιλονικεῖν πρὸς τὸ ἐμὲ εἶναι τὸν ἀποκρινόμενον.
τελευτῶν δὲ συνεχώρησεν, κἄπειτα, Αὕτη δή, ἔφη, b
ἡ Σωκράτους σοφία· αὐτὸν μὲν μὴ ἐθέλειν διδάσκειν,
παρὰ δὲ τῶν ἄλλων περιιόντα μανθάνειν καὶ τούτων
μηδὲ χάριν ἀποδιδόναι.

Ὅτι μέν, ἦν δ' ἐγώ, μανθάνω παρὰ τῶν ἄλλων, 5
ἀληθῆ εἶπες, ὦ Θρασύμαχε, ὅτι δὲ οὔ με φὴς χάριν
ἐκτίνειν, ψεύδῃ· ἐκτίνω γὰρ ὅσην δύναμαι. δύναμαι
δὲ ἐπαινεῖν μόνον· χρήματα γὰρ οὐκ ἔχω. ὡς δὲ

προθύμως τοῦτο δρῶ, ἐάν τίς μοι δοκῇ εὖ λέγειν, εὖ
10 εἴσῃ αὐτίκα δὴ μάλα, ἐπειδὰν ἀποκρίνῃ· οἶμαι γάρ
σε εὖ ἐρεῖν.

c ῎Ακουε δή, ἦ δ᾽ ὅς. φημὶ γὰρ ἐγὼ εἶναι τὸ δίκαιον
οὐκ ἄλλο τι ἢ τὸ τοῦ κρείττονος συμφέρον. ἀλλὰ τί
οὐκ ἐπαινεῖς; ἀλλ᾽ οὐκ ἐθελήσεις.

᾽Εὰν μάθω γε πρῶτον, ἔφην, τί λέγεις· νῦν γὰρ
5 οὔπω οἶδα. τὸ τοῦ κρείττονος φῂς συμφέρον δίκαιον
εἶναι. καὶ τοῦτο, ὦ Θρασύμαχε, τί ποτε λέγεις; οὐ
γάρ που τό γε τοιόνδε φῄς· εἰ Πουλυδάμας ἡμῶν
κρείττων ὁ παγκρατιαστὴς καὶ αὐτῷ συμφέρει τὰ
βόεια κρέα πρὸς τὸ σῶμα, τοῦτο τὸ σιτίον εἶναι καὶ
d ἡμῖν τοῖς ἥττοσιν ἐκείνου συμφέρον ἅμα καὶ δίκαιον.

Βδελυρὸς γὰρ εἶ, ἔφη, ὦ Σώκρατες, καὶ ταύτῃ
ὑπολαμβάνεις ᾗ ἂν κακουργήσαις μάλιστα τὸν
λόγον.

5 Οὐδαμῶς, ὦ ἄριστε, ἦν δ᾽ ἐγώ· ἀλλὰ σαφέστερον
εἰπὲ τί λέγεις.

Εἶτ᾽ οὐκ οἶσθ᾽, ἔφη, ὅτι τῶν πόλεων αἱ μὲν τυραν-
νοῦνται, αἱ δὲ δημοκρατοῦνται, αἱ δὲ ἀριστοκρατοῦνται;
Πῶς γὰρ οὔ;
10 Οὐκοῦν τοῦτο κρατεῖ ἐν ἑκάστῃ πόλει, τὸ ἄρχον;
Πάνυ γε.

e Τίθεται δέ γε τοὺς νόμους ἑκάστη ἡ ἀρχὴ πρὸς τὸ
αὑτῇ συμφέρον, δημοκρατία μὲν δημοκρατικούς,
τυραννὶς δὲ τυραννικούς, καὶ αἱ ἄλλαι οὕτως· θέμεναι
δὲ ἀπέφηναν τοῦτο δίκαιον τοῖς ἀρχομένοις εἶναι, τὸ
5 σφίσι συμφέρον, καὶ τὸν τούτου ἐκβαίνοντα κολάζουσιν
ὡς παρανομοῦντά τε καὶ ἀδικοῦντα. τοῦτ᾽ οὖν ἐστιν,
ὦ βέλτιστε, ὃ λέγω ἐν ἁπάσαις ταῖς πόλεσιν ταὐτὸν
339 εἶναι δίκαιον, τὸ τῆς καθεστηκυίας ἀρχῆς συμφέρον·
αὕτη δέ που κρατεῖ, ὥστε συμβαίνει τῷ ὀρθῶς

λογιζομένῳ πανταχοῦ εἶναι τὸ αὐτὸ δίκαιον, τὸ τοῦ κρείττονος συμφέρον.

Νῦν, ἦν δ᾽ ἐγώ, ἔμαθον ὃ λέγεις· εἰ δὲ ἀληθὲς ἢ 5 μή, πειράσομαι μαθεῖν. τὸ συμφέρον μὲν οὖν, ὦ Θρασύμαχε, καὶ σὺ ἀπεκρίνω δίκαιον εἶναι· καίτοι ἔμοιγε ἀπηγόρευες ὅπως μὴ τοῦτο ἀποκρινοίμην — πρόσεστιν δὲ δὴ αὐτόθι τὸ " τοῦ κρείττονος ".

Σμικρά γε ἴσως, ἔφη, προσθήκη.   b

Οὔπω δῆλον οὐδ᾽ εἰ μεγάλη· ἀλλ᾽ ὅτι μὲν τοῦτο σκεπτέον εἰ ἀληθῆ λέγεις, δῆλον. ἐπειδὴ γὰρ συμφέρον γέ τι εἶναι καὶ ἐγὼ ὁμολογῶ τὸ δίκαιον, σὺ δὲ προστιθεὶς καὶ αὐτὸ φῂς εἶναι τὸ τοῦ κρείττονος, ἐγὼ δὲ ἀγνοῶ, 5 σκεπτέον δή.

Σκόπει, ἔφη.

Ταῦτ᾽ ἔσται, ἦν δ᾽ ἐγώ. καί μοι εἰπέ· οὐ καὶ πείθεσθαι μέντοι τοῖς ἄρχουσιν δίκαιον φῂς εἶναι ;

Ἔγωγε.

Πότερον δὲ ἀναμάρτητοί εἰσιν οἱ ἄρχοντες ἐν ταῖς c πόλεσιν ἑκάσταις ἢ οἷοί τι καὶ ἁμαρτεῖν ;

Πάντως που, ἔφη, οἷοί τι καὶ ἁμαρτεῖν.

Οὐκοῦν ἐπιχειροῦντες νόμους τιθέναι τοὺς μὲν ὀρθῶς τιθέασιν, τοὺς δέ τινας οὐκ ὀρθῶς ;   5

Οἶμαι ἔγωγε.

Τὸ δὲ ὀρθῶς ἆρα τὸ τὰ συμφέροντά ἐστι τίθεσθαι ἑαυτοῖς, τὸ δὲ μὴ ὀρθῶς ἀσύμφορα ; ἢ πῶς λέγεις ;

Οὕτως.

Ἃ δ᾽ ἂν θῶνται ποιητέον τοῖς ἀρχομένοις, καὶ 10 τοῦτό ἐστι τὸ δίκαιον ;

Πῶς γὰρ οὔ ;

Οὐ μόνον ἄρα δίκαιόν ἐστιν κατὰ τὸν σὸν λόγον d τὸ τοῦ κρείττονος συμφέρον ποιεῖν ἀλλὰ καὶ τοὐναντίον τὸ μὴ συμφέρον.

Τί λέγεις σύ ; ἔφη.

5 ῍Α σὺ λέγεις, ἔμοιγε δοκῶ· σκοπῶμεν δὲ βέλτιον. οὐχ ὡμολόγηται τοὺς ἄρχοντας τοῖς ἀρχομένοις προστάττοντας ποιεῖν ἄττα ἐνίοτε διαμαρτάνειν τοῦ ἑαυτοῖς βελτίστου, ἃ δ᾽ ἂν προστάττωσιν οἱ ἄρχοντες δίκαιον εἶναι τοῖς ἀρχομένοις ποιεῖν ; ταῦτ᾽ οὐχ 10 ὡμολόγηται ;

Οἶμαι ἔγωγε, ἔφη.

e Οἴου τοίνυν, ἦν δ᾽ ἐγώ, καὶ τὸ ἀσύμφορα ποιεῖν τοῖς ἄρχουσί τε καὶ κρείττοσι δίκαιον εἶναι ὡμολογῆσθαί σοι, ὅταν οἱ μὲν ἄρχοντες ἄκοντες κακὰ αὑτοῖς προστάτ- τωσιν, τοῖς δὲ δίκαιον εἶναι φῇς ταῦτα ποιεῖν ἃ ἐκεῖνοι 5 προσέταξαν—ἆρα τότε, ὦ σοφώτατε Θρασύμαχε, οὐκ ἀναγκαῖον συμβαίνειν αὐτὸ οὑτωσί, δίκαιον εἶναι ποιεῖν τοὐναντίον ἢ ὃ σὺ λέγεις ; τὸ γὰρ τοῦ κρείτ- τονος ἀσύμφορον δήπου προστάττεται τοῖς ἥττοσιν ποιεῖν.

340 Ναὶ μὰ Δί᾽, ἔφη, ὦ Σώκρατες, ὁ Πολέμαρχος, σαφέστατά γε.

Ἐὰν σύ γ᾽, ἔφη, αὐτῷ μαρτυρήσῃς, ὁ Κλειτοφῶν ὑπολαβών.

5 Καὶ τί, ἔφη, δεῖται μάρτυρος ; αὐτὸς γὰρ Θρασύμαχος ὁμολογεῖ τοὺς μὲν ἄρχοντας ἐνίοτε ἑαυτοῖς κακὰ προστάττειν, τοῖς δ᾽ ἀρχομενοις δίκαιον εἶναι ταῦτα ποιεῖν.

Τὸ γὰρ τὰ κελευόμενα ποιεῖν, ὦ Πολέμαρχε, ὑπὸ 10 τῶν ἀρχόντων δίκαιον εἶναι ἔθετο Θρασύμαχος.

Καὶ γὰρ τὸ τοῦ κρείττονος, ὦ Κλειτοφῶν, συμφέρον b δίκαιον εἶναι ἔθετο. ταῦτα δὲ ἀμφότερα θέμενος ὡμολόγησεν αὖ ἐνίοτε τοὺς κρείττους τὰ αὑτοῖς ἀσύμφορα κελεύειν τοὺς ἥττους τε καὶ ἀρχομένους ποιεῖν. ἐκ δὲ τούτων τῶν ὁμολογιῶν οὐδὲν μᾶλλον

τὸ τοῦ κρείττονος συμφέρον δίκαιον ἂν εἴη ἢ τὸ μὴ 5
συμφέρον.

'Αλλ', ἔφη ὁ Κλειτοφῶν, τὸ τοῦ κρείττονος συμφέρον
ἔλεγεν ὃ ἡγοῖτο ὁ κρείττων αὑτῷ συμφέρειν· τοῦτο
ποιητέον εἶναι τῷ ἥττονι, καὶ τὸ δίκαιον τοῦτο ἐτίθετο.

'Αλλ' οὐχ οὕτως, ἦ δ' ὃς ὁ Πολέμαρχος, ἐλέγετο.   10

Οὐδέν, ἦν δ' ἐγώ, ὦ Πολέμαρχε, διαφέρει, ἀλλ' c
εἰ νῦν οὕτω λέγει Θρασύμαχος, οὕτως αὐτοῦ ἀποδε-
χώμεθα. Καί μοι εἰπέ, ὦ Θρασύμαχε· τοῦτο ἦν ὃ
ἐβούλου λέγειν τὸ δίκαιον, τὸ τοῦ κρείττονος συμφέρον
δοκοῦν εἶναι τῷ κρείττονι, ἐάντε συμφέρῃ ἐάντε μή ; 5
οὕτω σε φῶμεν λέγειν ;

"Ηκιστά γε, ἔφη· ἀλλὰ κρείττω με οἴει καλεῖν τὸν
ἐξαμαρτάνοντα ὅταν ἐξαμαρτάνῃ ;

"Εγωγε, εἶπον, ᾤμην σε τοῦτο λέγειν ὅτε τοὺς
ἄρχοντας ὡμολόγεις οὐκ ἀναμαρτήτους εἶναι ἀλλά τι 10
καὶ ἐξαμαρτάνειν.

Συκοφάντης γὰρ εἶ, ἔφη, ὦ Σώκρατες, ἐν τοῖς d
λόγοις· ἐπεὶ αὐτίκα ἰατρὸν καλεῖς σὺ τὸν ἐξαμαρτάνοντα
περὶ τοὺς κάμνοντας κατ' αὐτὸ τοῦτο ὃ ἐξαμαρτάνει ;
ἢ λογιστικόν, ὃς ἂν ἐν λογισμῷ ἁμαρτάνῃ, τότε ὅταν
ἁμαρτάνῃ, κατὰ ταύτην τὴν ἁμαρτίαν ; ἀλλ' οἶμαι 5
λέγομεν τῷ ῥήματι οὕτως, ὅτι ὁ ἰατρὸς ἐξήμαρτεν
καὶ ὁ λογιστὴς ἐξήμαρτεν καὶ ὁ γραμματιστής· τὸ δ'
οἶμαι ἕκαστος τούτων, καθ' ὅσον τοῦτ' ἔστιν ὃ προσαγο-
ρεύομεν αὐτόν, οὐδέποτε ἁμαρτάνει· ὥστε κατὰ τὸν e
ἀκριβῆ λόγον, ἐπειδὴ καὶ σὺ ἀκριβολογῇ, οὐδεὶς τῶν
δημιουργῶν ἁμαρτάνει. ἐπιλειπούσης γὰρ ἐπιστήμης
ὁ ἁμαρτάνων ἁμαρτάνει, ἐν ᾧ οὐκ ἔστι δημιουργός·
ὥστε δημιουργὸς ἢ σοφὸς ἢ ἄρχων οὐδεὶς ἁμαρτάνει 5
τότε ὅταν ἄρχων ᾖ, ἀλλὰ πᾶς γ' ἂν εἴποι ὅτι ὁ ἰατρὸς
ἥμαρτεν καὶ ὁ ἄρχων ἥμαρτεν. τοιοῦτον οὖν δή σοι

καὶ ἐμὲ ὑπόλαβε νυνδὴ ἀποκρίνεσθαι· τὸ δὲ ἀκριβέστατον
ἐκεῖνο τυγχάνει ὄν, τὸν ἄρχοντα, καθ᾽ ὅσον ἄρχων
341 ἐστίν, μὴ ἁμαρτάνειν, μὴ ἁμαρτάνοντα δὲ τὸ αὑτῷ
βέλτιστον τίθεσθαι, τοῦτο δὲ τῷ ἀρχομένῳ ποιητέον.
ὥστε ὅπερ ἐξ ἀρχῆς ἔλεγον δίκαιον λέγω, τὸ τοῦ
κρείττονος ποιεῖν συμφέρον.
5   Εἶεν, ἦν δ᾽ ἐγώ, ὦ Θρασύμαχε· δοκῶ σοι συκοφαντεῖν ;
Πάνυ μὲν οὖν, ἔφη.
Οἴει γάρ με ἐξ ἐπιβουλῆς ἐν τοῖς λόγοις κακουρ-
γοῦντά σε ἐρέσθαι ὡς ἠρόμην ;
Εὖ μὲν οὖν οἶδα, ἔφη. καὶ οὐδέν γέ σοι πλέον ἔσται·
b οὔτε γὰρ ἄν με λάθοις κακουργῶν, οὔτε μὴ λαθὼν
βιάσασθαι τῷ λόγῳ δύναιο.
Οὐδέ γ᾽ ἂν ἐπιχειρήσαιμι, ἦν δ᾽ ἐγώ, ὦ μακάριε.
ἀλλ᾽ ἵνα μὴ αὖθις ἡμῖν τοιοῦτον ἐγγένηται, διόρισαι
5 ποτέρως λέγεις τὸν ἄρχοντά τε καὶ τὸν κρείττονα,
τὸν ὡς ἔπος εἰπεῖν ἢ τὸν ἀκριβεῖ λόγῳ, ὃ νυνδὴ
ἔλεγες, οὗ τὸ συμφέρον κρείττονος ὄντος δίκαιον
ἔσται τῷ ἥττονι ποιεῖν.
Τὸν τῷ ἀκριβεστάτῳ, ἔφη, λόγῳ ἄρχοντα ὄντα.
10 πρὸς ταῦτα κακούργει καὶ συκοφάντει, εἴ τι δύνασαι—
οὐδέν σου παρίεμαι—ἀλλ᾽ οὐ μὴ οἷός τ᾽ ἦς.
c   Οἴει γὰρ ἄν με, εἶπον, οὕτω μανῆναι ὥστε ξυρεῖν
ἐπιχειρεῖν λέοντα καὶ συκοφαντεῖν Θρασύμαχον ;
Νῦν γοῦν, ἔφη, ἐπεχείρησας, οὐδὲν ὢν καὶ ταῦτα.
Ἄδην, ἦν δ᾽ ἐγώ, τῶν τοιούτων. ἀλλ᾽ εἰπέ μοι·
5 ὁ τῷ ἀκριβεῖ λόγῳ ἰατρός, ὃν ἄρτι ἔλεγες, πότερον
χρηματιστής ἐστιν ἢ τῶν καμνόντων θεραπευτής ;
καὶ λέγε τὸν τῷ ὄντι ἰατρὸν ὄντα.
Τῶν καμνόντων, ἔφη, θεραπευτής.
Τί δὲ κυβερνήτης ; ὁ ὀρθῶς κυβερνήτης ναυτῶν
10 ἄρχων ἐστὶν ἢ ναύτης ;

Ναυτῶν ἄρχων.

Οὐδὲν οἶμαι τοῦτο ὑπολογιστέον, ὅτι πλεῖ ἐν τῇ **d** νηί, οὐδ’ ἐστὶν κλητέος ναύτης· οὐ γὰρ κατὰ τὸ πλεῖν κυβερνήτης καλεῖται, ἀλλὰ κατὰ τὴν τέχνην καὶ τὴν τῶν ναυτῶν ἀρχήν.

Ἀληθῆ, ἔφη.   5

Οὐκοῦν ἑκάστῳ τούτων ἔστιν τι συμφέρον ;

Πάνυ γε.

Οὐ καὶ ἡ τέχνη, ἦν δ’ ἐγώ, ἐπὶ τούτῳ πέφυκεν, ἐπὶ τῷ τὸ συμφέρον ἑκάστῳ ζητεῖν τε καὶ ἐκπορίζειν ;

Ἐπὶ τούτῳ, ἔφη.   10

Ἆρ’ οὖν καὶ ἑκάστῃ τῶν τεχνῶν ἔστιν τι συμφέρον ἄλλο ἢ ὅτι μάλιστα τελέαν εἶναι ;

Πῶς τοῦτο ἐρωτᾷς ;   **e**

Ὥσπερ, ἔφην ἐγώ, εἴ με ἔροιο εἰ ἐξαρκεῖ σώματι εἶναι σώματι ἢ προσδεῖταί τινος, εἴποιμ’ ἂν ὅτι “ Παντάπασι μὲν οὖν προσδεῖται. διὰ ταῦτα καὶ ἡ τέχνη ἐστὶν ἡ ἰατρικὴ νῦν ηὑρημένη, ὅτι σῶμά 5 ἐστιν πονηρὸν καὶ οὐκ ἐξαρκεῖ αὐτῷ τοιούτῳ εἶναι. τούτῳ οὖν ὅπως ἐκπορίζῃ τὰ συμφέροντα, ἐπὶ τούτῳ παρεσκευάσθη ἡ τέχνη ”. ἢ ὀρθῶς σοι δοκῶ, ἔφην, ἂν εἰπεῖν οὕτω λέγων, ἢ οὔ ;

Ὀρθῶς, ἔφη.

Τί δὲ δή ; αὐτὴ ἡ ἰατρική ἐστιν πονηρά, ἢ ἄλλη **342** τις τέχνη ἔσθ’ ὅτι προσδεῖταί τινος ἀρετῆς—ὥσπερ ὀφθαλμοὶ ὄψεως καὶ ὦτα ἀκοῆς καὶ διὰ ταῦτα ἐπ’ αὐτοῖς δεῖ τινος τέχνης τῆς τὸ συμφέρον εἰς αὐτὰ ταῦτα σκεψομένης τε καὶ ἐκποριούσης—ἆρα καὶ ἐν 5 αὐτῇ τῇ τέχνῃ ἔνι τις πονηρία, καὶ δεῖ ἑκάστῃ τέχνῃ ἄλλης τέχνης ἥτις αὐτῇ τὸ συμφέρον σκέψεται, καὶ τῇ σκοπουμένῃ ἑτέρας αὖ τοιαύτης, καὶ τοῦτ’ ἐστιν ἀπέραντον ; ἢ αὐτὴ αὑτῇ τὸ συμφέρον σκέψεται ; **b**

ἢ οὔτε αὑτῆς οὔτε ἄλλης προσδεῖται ἐπὶ τὴν αὑτῆς
πονηρίαν τὸ συμφέρον σκοπεῖν· οὔτε γὰρ πονηρία
οὔτε ἁμαρτία οὐδεμία οὐδεμιᾷ τέχνῃ πάρεστιν, οὐδὲ
5 προσήκει τέχνῃ ἄλλῳ τὸ συμφέρον ζητεῖν ἢ ἐκείνῳ
οὗ τέχνη ἐστίν, αὐτὴ δὲ ἀβλαβὴς καὶ ἀκέραιός ἐστιν
ὀρθὴ οὖσα, ἕωσπερ ἂν ᾖ ἑκάστη ἀκριβὴς ὅλη ἥπερ
ἐστίν ; καὶ σκόπει ἐκείνῳ τῷ ἀκριβεῖ λόγῳ· οὕτως
ἢ ἄλλως ἔχει ;
10 Οὕτως, ἔφη, φαίνεται.
c Οὐκ ἄρα, ἦν δ᾽ ἐγώ, ἰατρικὴ ἰατρικῇ τὸ συμφέρον
σκοπεῖ ἀλλὰ σώματι.
Ναί, ἔφη.
Οὐδὲ ἱππικὴ ἱππικῇ ἀλλ᾽ ἵπποις· οὐδὲ ἄλλη
5 τέχνη οὐδεμία ἑαυτῇ—οὐδὲ γὰρ προσδεῖται—ἀλλ᾽
ἐκείνῳ οὗ τέχνη ἐστίν.
Φαίνεται, ἔφη, οὕτως.
Ἀλλὰ μήν, ὦ Θρασύμαχε, ἄρχουσί γε αἱ τέχναι
καὶ κρατοῦσιν ἐκείνου οὗπέρ εἰσιν τέχναι.
10 Συνεχώρησεν ἐνταῦθα καὶ μάλα μόγις.
Οὐκ ἄρα ἐπιστήμη γε οὐδεμία τὸ τοῦ κρείττονος
συμφέρον σκοπεῖ οὐδ᾽ ἐπιτάττει, ἀλλὰ τὸ τοῦ ἥττονός
d τε καὶ ἀρχομένου ὑπὸ ἑαυτῆς.
Συνωμολόγησε μὲν καὶ ταῦτα τελευτῶν, ἐπεχείρει
δὲ περὶ αὐτὰ μάχεσθαι· ἐπειδὴ δὲ ὡμολόγησεν,
Ἄλλο τι οὖν, ἦν δ᾽ ἐγώ, οὐδὲ ἰατρὸς οὐδείς, καθ᾽
5 ὅσον ἰατρός, τὸ τῷ ἰατρῷ συμφέρον σκοπεῖ οὐδ᾽
ἐπιτάττει, ἀλλὰ τὸ τῷ κάμνοντι ; ὡμολόγηται γὰρ
ὁ ἀκριβὴς ἰατρὸς σωμάτων εἶναι ἄρχων ἀλλ᾽ οὐ
χρηματιστής. ἢ οὐχ ὡμολόγηται ;
Συνέφη.
10 Οὐκοῦν καὶ ὁ κυβερνήτης ὁ ἀκριβὴς ναυτῶν εἶναι
ἄρχων ἀλλ᾽ οὐ ναύτης ;

'Ωμολόγηται.   e

Οὐκ ἄρα ὅ γε τοιοῦτος κυβερνήτης τε καὶ ἄρχων
τὸ τῷ κυβερνήτῃ συμφέρον σκέψεταί τε καὶ προστάξει,
ἀλλὰ τὸ τῷ ναύτῃ τε καὶ ἀρχομένῳ.

Συνέφησε μόγις.   5

Οὐκοῦν, ἦν δ' ἐγώ, ὦ Θρασύμαχε, οὐδὲ ἄλλος οὐδεὶς
ἐν οὐδεμιᾷ ἀρχῇ, καθ' ὅσον ἄρχων ἐστίν, τὸ αὑτῷ
συμφέρον σκοπεῖ οὐδ' ἐπιτάττει, ἀλλὰ τὸ τῷ ἀρχομένῳ
καὶ ᾧ ἂν αὐτὸς δημιουργῇ, καὶ πρὸς ἐκεῖνο βλέπων
καὶ τὸ ἐκείνῳ συμφέρον καὶ πρέπον, καὶ λέγει ἃ λέγει 10
καὶ ποιεῖ ἃ ποιεῖ ἅπαντα.

Ἐπειδὴ οὖν ἐνταῦθα ἦμεν τοῦ λόγου καὶ πᾶσι 343
καταφανὲς ἦν ὅτι ὁ τοῦ δικαίου λόγος εἰς τοὐναντίον
περιειστήκει, ὁ Θρασύμαχος ἀντὶ τοῦ ἀποκρίνεσθαι,
Εἰπέ μοι, ἔφη, ὦ Σώκρατες, τίτθη σοι ἔστιν;

Τί δέ; ἦν δ' ἐγώ· οὐκ ἀποκρίνεσθαι χρῆν μᾶλλον 5
ἢ τοιαῦτα ἐρωτᾶν;

Ὅτι τοί σε, ἔφη, κορυζῶντα περιορᾷ, καὶ οὐκ
ἀπομύττει δεόμενον, ὅς γε αὐτῇ οὐδὲ πρόβατα οὐδὲ
ποιμένα γιγνώσκεις.

Ὅτι δὴ τί μάλιστα; ἦν δ' ἐγώ.   10

Ὅτι οἴει τοὺς ποιμένας ἢ τοὺς βουκόλους τὸ τῶν b
προβάτων ἢ τὸ τῶν βοῶν ἀγαθὸν σκοπεῖν καὶ παχύνειν
αὐτοὺς καὶ θεραπεύειν πρὸς ἄλλο τι βλέποντας ἢ τὸ
τῶν δεσποτῶν ἀγαθὸν καὶ τὸ αὐτῶν, καὶ δὴ καὶ τοὺς
ἐν ταῖς πόλεσιν ἄρχοντας, οἳ ὡς ἀληθῶς ἄρχουσιν, 5
ἄλλως πως ἡγῇ διανοεῖσθαι πρὸς τοὺς ἀρχομένους
ἢ ὥσπερ ἄν τις πρὸς πρόβατα διατεθείη, καὶ ἄλλο
τι σκοπεῖν αὐτοὺς διὰ νυκτὸς καὶ ἡμέρας ἢ τοῦτο,
ὅθεν αὐτοὶ ὠφελήσονται. καὶ οὕτω πόρρω εἶ περί c
τε τοῦ δικαίου καὶ δικαιοσύνης καὶ ἀδίκου τε καὶ
ἀδικίας, ὥστε ἀγνοεῖς ὅτι ἡ μὲν δικαιοσύνη καὶ τὸ

δίκαιον ἀλλότριον ἀγαθὸν, τῷ ὄντι τοῦ κρείττονός τε
5 καὶ ἄρχοντος συμφέρον, οἰκεία δὲ τοῦ πειθομένου τε
καὶ ὑπηρετοῦντος βλάβη, ἡ δὲ ἀδικία τοὐναντίον, καὶ
ἄρχει τῶν ὡς ἀληθῶς εὐηθικῶν τε καὶ δικαίων, οἱ
δ' ἀρχόμενοι ποιοῦσιν τὸ ἐκείνου συμφέρον κρείττονος
ὄντος, καὶ εὐδαίμονα ἐκεῖνον ποιοῦσιν ὑπηρετοῦντες
d αὐτῷ, ἑαυτοὺς δὲ οὐδ' ὁπωστιοῦν. σκοπεῖσθαι δέ,
ὦ εὐηθέστατε Σώκρατες, οὑτωσὶ χρή, ὅτι δίκαιος
ἀνὴρ ἀδίκου πανταχοῦ ἔλαττον ἔχει. πρῶτον μὲν ἐν
τοῖς πρὸς ἀλλήλους συμβολαίοις, ὅπου ἂν ὁ τοιοῦτος
5 τῷ τοιούτῳ κοινωνήσῃ, οὐδαμοῦ ἂν εὕροις ἐν τῇ
διαλύσει τῆς κοινωνίας πλέον ἔχοντα τὸν δίκαιον τοῦ
ἀδίκου ἀλλ' ἔλαττον· ἔπειτα ἐν τοῖς πρὸς τὴν πόλιν,
ὅταν τέ τινες εἰσφοραὶ ὦσιν, ὁ μὲν δίκαιος ἀπὸ τῶν
ἴσων πλέον εἰσφέρει, ὁ δ' ἔλαττον, ὅταν τε λήψεις,
e ὁ μὲν οὐδέν, ὁ δὲ πολλὰ κερδαίνει. καὶ γὰρ ὅταν
ἀρχήν τινα ἄρχῃ ἑκάτερος, τῷ μὲν δικαίῳ ὑπάρχει,
καὶ εἰ μηδεμία ἄλλη ζημία, τά γε οἰκεῖα δι' ἀμέλειαν
μοχθηροτέρως ἔχειν, ἐκ δὲ τοῦ δημοσίου μηδὲν
5 ὠφελεῖσθαι διὰ τὸ δίκαιον εἶναι, πρὸς δὲ τούτοις
ἀπεχθέσθαι τοῖς τε οἰκείοις καὶ τοῖς γνωρίμοις, ὅταν
μηδὲν ἐθέλῃ αὐτοῖς ὑπηρετεῖν παρὰ τὸ δίκαιον· τῷ
δὲ ἀδίκῳ πάντα τούτων τἀναντία ὑπάρχει. λέγω γὰρ
344 ὅνπερ νυνδὴ ἔλεγον, τὸν μεγάλα δυνάμενον πλεονεκτεῖν·
τοῦτον οὖν σκόπει, εἴπερ βούλει κρίνειν ὅσῳ μᾶλλον
συμφέρει ἰδίᾳ αὐτῷ ἄδικον εἶναι ἢ τὸ δίκαιον. πάντων
δὲ ῥᾷστα μαθήσῃ, ἐὰν ἐπὶ τὴν τελεωτάτην ἀδικίαν
5 ἔλθῃς, ἢ τὸν μὲν ἀδικήσαντα εὐδαιμονέστατον ποιεῖ,
τοὺς δὲ ἀδικηθέντας καὶ ἀδικῆσαι οὐκ ἂν ἐθέλοντας
ἀθλιωτάτους. ἔστιν δὲ τοῦτο τυραννίς, ἣ οὐ κατὰ
σμικρὸν τἀλλότρια καὶ λάθρᾳ καὶ βίᾳ ἀφαιρεῖται, καὶ
ἱερὰ καὶ ὅσια καὶ ἴδια καὶ δημόσια, ἀλλὰ συλλήβδην·

ὧν ἐφ' ἑκάστῳ μέρει ὅταν τις ἀδικήσας μὴ λάθῃ, b
ζημιοῦταί τε καὶ ὀνείδη ἔχει τὰ μέγιστα—καὶ γὰρ
ἱερόσυλοι καὶ ἀνδραποδισταὶ καὶ τοιχωρύχοι καὶ
ἀποστερηταὶ καὶ κλέπται οἱ κατὰ μέρη ἀδικοῦντες
τῶν τοιούτων κακουργημάτων καλοῦνται—ἐπειδὰν δέ 5
τις πρὸς τοῖς τῶν πολιτῶν χρήμασιν καὶ αὐτοὺς
ἀνδραποδισάμενος δουλώσηται, ἀντὶ τούτων τῶν
αἰσχρῶν ὀνομάτων εὐδαίμονες καὶ μακάριοι κέκληνται,
οὐ μόνον ὑπὸ τῶν πολιτῶν ἀλλὰ καὶ ὑπὸ τῶν ἄλλων c
ὅσοι ἂν πύθωνται αὐτὸν τὴν ὅλην ἀδικίαν ἠδικηκότα·
οὐ γὰρ τὸ ποιεῖν τὰ ἄδικα ἀλλὰ τὸ πάσχειν φοβούμενοι
ὀνειδίζουσιν οἱ ὀνειδίζοντες τὴν ἀδικίαν. οὕτως, ὦ
Σώκρατες, καὶ ἰσχυρότερον καὶ ἐλευθεριώτερον καὶ 5
δεσποτικώτερον ἀδικία δικαιοσύνης ἐστὶν ἱκανῶς
γιγνομένη, καὶ ὅπερ ἐξ ἀρχῆς ἔλεγον, τὸ μέν τοῦ
κρείττονος συμφέρον τὸ δίκαιον τυγχάνει ὄν, τὸ δ'
ἄδικον ἑαυτῷ λυσιτελοῦν τε καὶ συμφέρον.

Ταῦτα εἰπὼν ὁ Θρασύμαχος ἐν νῷ εἶχεν ἀπιέναι, d
ὥσπερ βαλανεὺς ἡμῶν καταντλήσας κατὰ τῶν ὤτων
ἀθρόον καὶ πολὺν τὸν λόγον· οὐ μὴν εἴασάν γε αὐτὸν
οἱ παρόντες, ἀλλ' ἠνάγκασαν ὑπομεῖναί τε καὶ παρασχεῖν
τῶν εἰρημένων λόγον. καὶ δὴ ἔγωγε καὶ αὐτὸς πάνυ 5
ἐδεόμην τε καὶ εἶπον· Ὦ δαιμόνιε Θρασύμαχε,
οἷον ἐμβαλὼν λόγον ἐν νῷ ἔχεις ἀπιέναι πρὶν διδάξαι
ἱκανῶς ἢ μαθεῖν εἴτε οὕτως εἴτε ἄλλως ἔχει; ἢ
σμικρὸν οἴει ἐπιχειρεῖν πρᾶγμα διορίζεσθαι ἀλλ' οὐ e
βίου διαγωγήν, ᾗ ἂν διαγόμενος ἕκαστος ἡμῶν λυσιτελε-
στάτην ζωὴν ζῴη;

Ἐγὼ γὰρ οἶμαι, ἔφη ὁ Θρασύμαχος, τουτὶ ἄλλως
ἔχειν;   5

Ἔοικας, ἦν δ' ἐγώ—ἤτοι ἡμῶν γε οὐδὲν κήδεσθαι,
οὐδέ τι φροντίζειν εἴτε χεῖρον εἴτε βέλτιον βιωσόμεθα

ἀγνοοῦντες ὃ σὺ φὴς εἰδέναι. ἀλλ', ὦγαθέ, προθυμοῦ
345 καὶ ἡμῖν ἐνδείξασθαι—οὔτοι κακῶς σοι κείσεται ὅτι
ἂν ἡμᾶς τοσούσδε ὄντας εὐεργετήσῃς—ἐγὼ γὰρ δή
σοι λέγω τό γ' ἐμόν, ὅτι οὐ πείθομαι οὐδ' οἶμαι ἀδικίαν
δικαιοσύνης κερδαλεώτερον εἶναι, οὐδ' ἐὰν ἐᾷ τις
5 αὐτὴν καὶ μὴ διακωλύῃ πράττειν ἃ βούλεται. ἀλλ',
ὦγαθέ, ἔστω μὲν ἄδικος, δυνάσθω δὲ ἀδικεῖν ἢ τῷ
λανθάνειν ἢ τῷ διαμάχεσθαι, ὅμως ἐμέ γε οὐ πείθει
ὡς ἔστι τῆς δικαιοσύνης κερδαλεώτερον. ταῦτ' οὖν
b καὶ ἕτερος ἴσως τις ἡμῶν πέπονθεν, οὐ μόνος ἐγώ·
πεῖσον οὖν, ὦ μακάριε, ἱκανῶς ἡμᾶς ὅτι οὐκ ὀρθῶς
βουλευόμεθα δικαιοσύνην ἀδικίας περὶ πλείονος
ποιούμενοι.

5 Καὶ πῶς, ἔφη, σὲ πείσω ; εἰ γὰρ οἷς νυνδὴ ἔλεγον
μὴ πέπεισαι, τί σοι ἔτι ποιήσω ; ἢ εἰς τὴν ψυχὴν
φέρων ἐνθῶ τὸν λόγον ;

Μὰ Δί', ἦν δ' ἐγώ, μὴ σύ γε· ἀλλὰ πρῶτον μέν,
ἃ ἂν εἴπῃς, ἔμμενε τούτοις, ἢ ἐὰν μετατιθῇ, φανερῶς
10 μετατίθεσο καὶ ἡμᾶς μὴ ἐξαπάτα. νῦν δὲ ὁρᾷς, ὦ
c Θρασύμαχε—ἔτι γὰρ τὰ ἔμπροσθεν ἐπισκεψώμεθα—
ὅτι τὸν ὡς ἀληθῶς ἰατρὸν τὸ πρῶτον ὁριζόμενος τὸν
ὡς ἀληθῶς ποιμένα οὐκέτι ᾤου δεῖν ὕστερον ἀκριβῶς
φυλάξαι, ἀλλὰ πιαίνειν οἴει αὐτὸν τὰ πρόβατα, καθ'
5 ὅσον ποιμήν ἐστιν, οὐ πρὸς τὸ τῶν προβάτων βέλτιστον
βλέποντα ἀλλ', ὥσπερ δαιτυμόνα τινὰ καὶ μέλλοντα
ἑστιάσεσθαι, πρὸς τὴν εὐωχίαν, ἢ αὖ πρὸς τὸ ἀποδόσθαι,
d ὥσπερ χρηματιστὴν ἀλλ' οὐ ποιμένα. τῇ δὲ ποιμενικῇ
οὐ δήπου ἄλλου του μέλει ἢ ἐφ' ᾧ τέτακται, ὅπως
τούτῳ τὸ βέλτιστον ἐκποριεῖ—ἐπεὶ τά γε αὐτῆς ὥστ'
εἶναι βελτίστη ἱκανῶς δήπου ἐκπεπόρισται, ἕως γ'
5 ἂν μηδὲν ἐνδέῃ τοῦ ποιμενικὴ εἶναι—οὕτω δὲ ᾤμην
ἔγωγε νυνδὴ ἀναγκαῖον εἶναι ἡμῖν ὁμολογεῖν πᾶσαν

ἀρχήν, καθ' ὅσον ἀρχή, μηδενὶ ἄλλῳ τὸ βέλτιστον
σκοπεῖσθαι ἢ ἐκείνῳ, τῷ ἀρχομένῳ τε καὶ θεραπευομένῳ, e
ἔν τε πολιτικῇ καὶ ἰδιωτικῇ ἀρχῇ. σὺ δὲ τοὺς
ἄρχοντας ἐν ταῖς πόλεσιν, τοὺς ὡς ἀληθῶς ἄρχοντας,
ἑκόντας οἴει ἄρχειν ;

Μὰ Δί' οὔκ, ἔφη, ἀλλ' εὖ οἶδα. 5

Τί δέ, ἦν δ' ἐγώ, ὦ Θρασύμαχε ; τὰς ἄλλας ἀρχὰς
οὐκ ἐννοεῖς ὅτι οὐδεὶς ἐθέλει ἄρχειν ἑκών, ἀλλὰ μισθὸν
αἰτοῦσιν, ὡς οὐχὶ αὐτοῖσιν ὠφελίαν ἐσομένην ἐκ τοῦ
ἄρχειν ἀλλὰ τοῖς ἀρχομένοις ; ἐπεὶ τοσόνδε εἰπέ· 346
οὐχὶ ἑκάστην μέντοι φαμὲν ἑκάστοτε τῶν τεχνῶν
τούτῳ ἑτέραν εἶναι, τῷ ἑτέραν τὴν δύναμιν ἔχειν ;
καί, ὦ μακάριε, μὴ παρὰ δόξαν ἀποκρίνου, ἵνα τι
καὶ περαίνωμεν. 5

Ἀλλὰ τούτῳ, ἔφη, ἑτέρα.

Οὐκοῦν καὶ ὠφελίαν ἑκάστη ἰδίαν τινὰ ἡμῖν παρέ-
χεται ἀλλ' οὐ κοινήν, οἷον ἰατρικὴ μὲν ὑγίειαν, κυβερνη-
τικὴ δὲ σωτηρίαν ἐν τῷ πλεῖν, καὶ αἱ ἄλλαι οὕτω ;

Πάνυ γε.

Οὐκοῦν καὶ μισθωτικὴ μισθόν ; αὕτη γὰρ αὐτῆς b
ἡ δύναμις· ἢ τὴν ἰατρικὴν σὺ καὶ τὴν κυβερνητικὴν
τὴν αὐτὴν καλεῖς ; ἢ ἐάνπερ βούλῃ ἀκριβῶς διορίζειν,
ὥσπερ ὑπέθου, οὐδέν τι μᾶλλον, ἐάν τις κυβερνῶν
ὑγιὴς γίγνηται διὰ τὸ συμφέρον αὐτῷ πλεῖν ἐν τῇ 5
θαλάττῃ, ἕνεκα τούτου καλεῖς μᾶλλον αὐτὴν ἰατκριήν ;

Οὐ δῆτα, ἔφη.

Οὐδέ γ', οἶμαι, τὴν μισθωτικήν, ἐὰν ὑγιαίνῃ τις
μισθαρνῶν.

Οὐ δῆτα. 10

Τί δέ ; τὴν ἰατρικὴν μισθαρνητικήν, ἐὰν ἰώμενός τις
μισθαρνῇ ;

Οὐκ ἔφη. c

Οὐκοῦν τήν γε ὠφελίαν ἑκάστης τῆς τέχνης ἰδίαν ὡμολογήσαμεν εἶναι ;

Ἔστω, ἔφη.

5 Ἥντινα ἄρα ὠφελίαν κοινῇ ὠφελοῦνται πάντες οἱ δημιουργοί, δῆλον ὅτι κοινῇ τινι τῷ αὐτῷ προσχρώμενοι ἀπ' ἐκείνου ὠφελοῦνται.

Ἔοικεν, ἔφη.

Φαμὲν δέ γε τὸ μισθὸν ἀρνυμένους ὠφελεῖσθαι τοὺς
10 δημιουργοὺς ἀπὸ τοῦ προσχρῆσθαι τῇ μισθωτικῇ τέχνῃ γίγνεσθαι αὐτοῖς.

Συνέφη μόγις.

d Οὐκ ἄρα ἀπὸ τῆς αὐτοῦ τέχνης ἑκάστῳ αὕτη ἡ ὠφελία ἐστίν, ἡ τοῦ μισθοῦ λῆψις, ἀλλ', εἰ δεῖ ἀκριβῶς σκοπεῖσθαι, ἡ μὲν ἰατρικὴ ὑγίειαν ποιεῖ, ἡ δὲ μισθαρνητικὴ μισθόν, καὶ ἡ μὲν οἰκοδομικὴ οἰκίαν, ἡ δὲ
5 μισθαρνητικὴ αὐτῇ ἑπομένη μισθόν, καὶ αἱ ἄλλαι πᾶσαι οὕτως τὸ αὑτῆς ἑκάστη ἔργον ἐργάζεται καὶ ὠφελεῖ ἐκεῖνο ἐφ' ᾧ τέτακται. ἐὰν δὲ μὴ μισθὸς αὐτῇ προσγίγνηται, ἔσθ' ὅτι ὠφελεῖται ὁ δημιουργὸς ἀπὸ τῆς τέχνης ;

10 Οὐ φαίνεται, ἔφη.

e Ἆρ' οὖν οὐδ' ὠφελεῖ τότε, ὅταν προῖκα ἐργάζηται ;

Οἶμαι ἔγωγε.

Οὐκοῦν, ὦ Θρασύμαχε, τοῦτο ἤδη δῆλον, ὅτι οὐδεμία τέχνη οὐδὲ ἀρχὴ τὸ αὑτῇ ὠφέλιμον παρα-
5 σκευάζει, ἀλλ', ὅπερ πάλαι ἐλέγομεν, τὸ τῷ ἀρχομένῳ καὶ παρασκευάζει καὶ ἐπιτάττει, τὸ ἐκείνου συμφέρον ἥττονος ὄντος σκοποῦσα, ἀλλ' οὐ τὸ τοῦ κρείττονος. διὰ δὴ ταῦτα ἔγωγε, ὦ φίλε Θρασύμαχε, καὶ ἄρτι ἔλεγον μηδένα ἐθέλειν ἑκόντα ἄρχειν καὶ τὰ ἀλλότρια
10 κακὰ μεταχειρίζεσθαι ἀνορθοῦντα, ἀλλὰ μισθὸν αἰτεῖν,
347 ὅτι ὁ μέλλων καλῶς τῇ τέχνῃ πράξειν οὐδέποτε

αὐτῷ τὸ βέλτιστον πράττει οὐδ' ἐπιτάττει κατὰ τὴν
τέχνην ἐπιτάττων, ἀλλὰ τῷ ἀρχομένῳ· ὧν δὴ ἕνεκα,
ὡς ἔοικε, μισθὸν δεῖν ὑπάρχειν τοῖς μέλλουσιν ἐθελήσειν
ἄρχειν, ἢ ἀργύριον ἢ τιμήν, ἢ ζημίαν ἐὰν μὴ ἄρχῃ. 5

Πῶς τοῦτο λέγεις, ὦ Σώκρατες ; ἔφη ὁ Γλαύκων·
τοὺς μὲν γὰρ δύο μισθοὺς γιγνώσκω, τὴν δὲ ζημίαν
ἥντινα λέγεις καὶ ὡς ἐν μισθοῦ μέρει εἴρηκας, οὐ
συνῆκα.

Τὸν τῶν βελτίστων ἄρα μισθόν, ἔφην, οὐ συνιεῖς, 10
δι' ὃν ἄρχουσιν οἱ ἐπιεικέστατοι, ὅταν ἐθέλωσιν ἄρχειν. b
ἢ οὐκ οἶσθα ὅτι τὸ φιλότιμόν τε καὶ φιλάργυρον
εἶναι ὄνειδος λέγεταί τε καὶ ἔστιν ;

Ἔγωγε, ἔφη.

Διὰ ταῦτα τοίνυν, ἦν δ' ἐγώ, οὔτε χρημάτων ἕνεκα 5
ἐθέλουσιν ἄρχειν οἱ ἀγαθοὶ οὔτε τιμῆς· οὔτε γὰρ
φανερῶς πραττόμενοι τῆς ἀρχῆς ἕνεκα μισθὸν μισθωτοὶ
βούλονται κεκλῆσθαι, οὔτε λάθρα αὐτοὶ ἐκ τῆς ἀρχῆς
λαμβάνοντες κλέπται. οὐδ' αὖ τιμῆς ἕνεκα· οὐ γάρ
εἰσι φιλότιμοι. δεῖ δὴ αὐτοῖς ἀνάγκην προσεῖναι καὶ c
ζημίαν, εἰ μέλλουσιν ἐθέλειν ἄρχειν—ὅθεν κινδυνεύει
τὸ ἑκόντα ἐπὶ τὸ ἄρχειν ἰέναι ἀλλὰ μὴ ἀνάγκην περιμένειν
αἰσχρὸν νενομίσθαι—τῆς δὲ ζημίας μεγίστη τὸ ὑπὸ
πονηροτέρου ἄρχεσθαι, ἐὰν μὴ αὐτὸς ἐθέλῃ ἄρχειν· 5
ἣν δείσαντές μοι φαίνονται ἄρχειν, ὅταν ἄρχωσιν, οἱ
ἐπιεικεῖς, καὶ τότε ἔρχονται ἐπὶ τὸ ἄρχειν οὐχ ὡς
ἐπ' ἀγαθόν τι ἰόντες οὐδ' ὡς εὐπαθήσοντες ἐν αὐτῷ,
ἀλλ' ὡς ἐπ' ἀναγκαῖον καὶ οὐκ ἔχοντες ἑαυτῶν βελτίοσιν d
ἐπιτρέψαι οὐδὲ ὁμοίοις. ἐπεὶ κινδυνεύει, πόλις ἀνδρῶν
ἀγαθῶν εἰ γένοιτο, περιμάχητον ἂν εἶναι τὸ μὴ ἄρχειν
ὥσπερ νυνὶ τὸ ἄρχειν, καὶ ἐνταῦθ' ἂν καταφανὲς
γενέσθαι ὅτι τῷ ὄντι ἀληθινὸς ἄρχων οὐ πέφυκε τὸ 5
αὐτῷ συμφέρον σκοπεῖσθαι ἀλλὰ τὸ τῷ ἀρχομένῳ·

ὥστε πᾶς ἂν ὁ γιγνώσκων τὸ ὠφελεῖσθαι μᾶλλον
ἕλοιτο ὑπ' ἄλλου ἢ ἄλλον ὠφελῶν πράγματα ἔχειν.
τοῦτο μὲν οὖν ἔγωγε οὐδαμῇ συγχωρῶ Θρασυμάχῳ,
e ὡς τὸ δίκαιόν ἐστιν τὸ τοῦ κρείττονος συμφέρον.
ἀλλὰ τοῦτο μὲν δὴ καὶ εἰς αὖθις σκεψόμεθα· πολὺ
δέ μοι δοκεῖ μεῖζον εἶναι ὃ νῦν λέγει Θρασύμαχος,
τὸν τοῦ ἀδίκου βίον φάσκων εἶναι κρείττω ἢ τὸν τοῦ
5 δικαίου. σὺ οὖν ποτέρως, ἦν δ' ἐγώ, ὦ Γλαύκων,
αἱρῇ ; καὶ πότερον ἀληθεστέρως δοκεῖ σοι λέγεσθαι ;
   Τὸν τοῦ δικαίου ἔγωγε, ἔφη, λυσιτελέστερον βίον εἶναι.
348 Ἤκουσας, ἦν δ' ἐγώ, ὅσα ἄρτι Θρασύμαχος ἀγαθὰ
διῆλθεν τῷ τοῦ ἀδίκου ;
   Ἤκουσα, ἔφη, ἀλλ' οὐ πείθομαι.
   Βούλει οὖν αὐτὸν πείθωμεν, ἂν δυνώμεθά πῃ ἐξευρεῖν,
5 ὡς οὐκ ἀληθῆ λέγει ;
   Πῶς γὰρ οὐ βούλομαι ; ἦ δ' ὅς.
   Ἂν μὲν τοίνυν, ἦν δ' ἐγώ, ἀντικατατείναντες λέγωμεν
αὐτῷ λόγον παρὰ λόγον, ὅσα αὖ ἀγαθὰ ἔχει τὸ δίκαιον
εἶναι, καὶ αὖθις οὗτος, καὶ ἄλλον ἡμεῖς, ἀριθμεῖν δεήσει
b τἀγαθὰ καὶ μετρεῖν ὅσα ἑκάτεροι ἐν ἑκατέρῳ λέγομεν,
καὶ ἤδη δικαστῶν τινων τῶν διακρινούντων δεησόμεθα·
ἂν δὲ ὥσπερ ἄρτι ἀνομολογούμενοι πρὸς ἀλλήλους
σκοπῶμεν, ἅμα αὐτοί τε δικασταὶ καὶ ῥήτορες ἐσόμεθα.
5 Πάνυ μὲν οὖν, ἔφη.
   Ὁποτέρως οὖν σοι, ἦν δ' ἐγώ, ἀρέσκει.
   Οὕτως, ἔφη.
   Ἴθι δή, ἦν δ' ἐγώ, ὦ Θρασύμαχε, ἀπόκριναι ἡμῖν
ἐξ ἀρχῆς. τὴν τελέαν ἀδικίαν τελέας οὔσης δικαιοσύνης
10 λυσιτελεστέραν φὴς εἶναι ;
c Πάνυ μὲν οὖν καὶ φημί, ἔφη, καὶ δι' ἅ, εἴρηκα.
   Φέρε δή, τὸ τοιόνδε περὶ αὐτῶν πῶς λέγεις ;
τὸ μέν που ἀρετὴν αὐτοῖν καλεῖς, τὸ δὲ κακίαν ;

Πῶς γὰρ οὔ ;

Οὐκοῦν τὴν μὲν δικαιοσύνην ἀρετήν, τὴν δὲ ἀδικίαν 5
κακίαν ;

Εἰκός γ᾽, ἔφη, ὦ ἥδιστε, ἐπειδή γε καὶ λέγω ἀδικίαν
μὲν λυσιτελεῖν, δικαιοσύνην δ᾽ οὔ.

᾽Αλλὰ τί μήν ;

Τοὐναντίον, ἦ δ᾽ ὅς.   10

῍Η τὴν δικαιοσύνην κακίαν ;

Οὔκ, ἀλλὰ πάνυ γενναίαν εὐήθειαν.

Τὴν ἀδικίαν ἄρα κακοήθειαν καλεῖς ;   d

Οὔκ, ἀλλ᾽ εὐβουλίαν, ἔφη.

῍Η καὶ φρόνιμοί σοι, ὦ Θρασύμαχε, δοκοῦσιν εἶναι
καὶ ἀγαθοὶ οἱ ἄδικοι ;

Οἵ γε τελέως, ἔφη, οἷοί τε ἀδικεῖν, πόλεις τε καὶ 5
ἔθνη δυνάμενοι ἀνθρώπων ὑφ᾽ ἑαυτοὺς ποιεῖσθαι· σὺ
δὲ οἴει με ἴσως τοὺς τὰ βαλλάντια ἀποτέμνοντας
λέγειν. λυσιτελεῖ μὲν οὖν, ἦ δ᾽ ὅς, καὶ τὰ τοιαῦτα,
ἐάνπερ λανθάνῃ· ἔστι δὲ οὐκ ἄξια λόγου, ἀλλ᾽ ἃ
νυνδὴ ἔλεγον.   10

Τοῦτο μέν, ἔφην, οὐκ ἀγνοῶ ὅ τι βούλει λέγειν, e
ἀλλὰ τόδε ἐθαύμασα, εἰ ἐν ἀρετῆς καὶ σοφίας τιθεῖς
μέρει τὴν ἀδικίαν, τὴν δὲ δικαιοσύνην ἐν τοῖς ἐναντίοις.

᾽Αλλὰ πάνυ οὕτω τίθημι.

Τοῦτο, ἦν δ᾽ ἐγώ, ἤδη στερεώτερον, ὦ ἑταῖρε, καὶ 5
οὐκέτι ῥᾴδιον ἔχειν ὅτι τις εἴπῃ. εἰ γὰρ λυσιτελεῖν
μὲν τὴν ἀδικίαν ἐτίθεσο, κακίαν μέντοι ἢ αἰσχρὸν
αὐτὸ ὡμολόγεις εἶναι ὥσπερ ἄλλοι τινές, εἴχομεν ἄν
τι λέγειν κατὰ τὰ νομιζόμενα λέγοντες· νῦν δὲ δῆλος
εἶ ὅτι φήσεις αὐτὸ καὶ καλὸν καὶ ἰσχυρὸν εἶναι καὶ 10
τἆλλα αὐτῷ πάντα προσθήσεις ἃ ἡμεῖς τῷ δικαίῳ
προσετίθεμεν, ἐπειδή γε καὶ ἐν ἀρετῇ αὐτὸ καὶ σοφίᾳ 349
ἐτόλμησας θεῖναι.

Ἀληθέστατα, ἔφη, μαντεύῃ.

Ἀλλ' οὐ μέντοι, ἦν δ' ἐγώ, ἀποκνητέον γε τῷ
5 λόγῳ ἐπεξελθεῖν σκοπούμενον, ἕως ἄν σε ὑπολαμβάνω
λέγειν ἅπερ διανοῇ. ἐμοὶ γὰρ δοκεῖς σύ, ὦ
Θρασύμαχε, ἀτεχνῶς νῦν οὐ σκώπτειν, ἀλλὰ τὰ
δοκοῦντα περὶ τῆς ἀληθείας λέγειν.

Τί δέ σοι, ἔφη, τοῦτο διαφέρει, εἴτε μοι δοκεῖ εἴτε
10 μή, ἀλλ' οὐ τὸν λόγον ἐλέγχεις ;

b   Οὐδέν, ἦν δ' ἐγώ. ἀλλὰ τόδε μοι πειρῶ ἔτι πρὸς
τούτοις ἀποκρίνασθαι· ὁ δίκαιος τοῦ δικαίου δοκεῖ
τί σοι ἂν ἐθέλειν πλέον ἔχειν ;

Οὐδαμῶς, ἔφη· οὐ γὰρ ἂν ἦν ἀστεῖος, ὥσπερ νῦν,
5 καὶ εὐήθης.

Τί δέ ; τῆς δικαίας πράξεως ;

Οὐδὲ τῆς δικαίας, ἔφη.

Τοῦ δὲ ἀδίκου πότερον ἀξιοῖ ἂν πλεονεκτεῖν καὶ
ἡγοῖτο δίκαιον εἶναι, ἢ οὐκ ἂν ἡγοῖτο ;

10 Ἡγοῖτ' ἄν, ἦ δ' ὅς, καὶ ἀξιοῖ, ἀλλ' οὐκ ἂν δύναιτο.

Ἀλλ' οὐ τοῦτο, ἦν δ' ἐγώ, ἐρωτῶ, ἀλλ' εἰ τοῦ
c μὲν δικαίου μὴ ἀξιοῖ πλέον ἔχειν μηδὲ βούλεται ὁ
δίκαιος, τοῦ δὲ ἀδίκου ;

Ἀλλ' οὕτως, ἔφη, ἔχει.

Τί δὲ δὴ ὁ ἄδικος ; ἆρα ἀξιοῖ τοῦ δικαίου πλεονεκτεῖν
5 καὶ τῆς δικαίας πράξεως ;

Πῶς γὰρ οὔκ ; ἔφη, ὅς γε πάντων πλέον ἔχειν ἀξιοῖ ;

Οὐκοῦν καὶ ἀδίκου ἀνθρώπου τε καὶ πράξεως ὁ
ἄδικος πλεονεκτήσει καὶ ἁμιλλήσεται ὡς ἁπάντων
πλεῖστον αὐτὸς λάβῃ ;

10 Ἔστι ταῦτα.

Ὧδε δὴ λέγωμεν, ἔφην· ὁ δίκαιος τοῦ μὲν ὁμοίου
οὐ πλεονεκτεῖ, τοῦ δὲ ἀνομοίου, ὁ δὲ ἄδικος τοῦ τε
d ὁμοίου καὶ τοῦ ἀνομοίου ;

Ἄριστα, ἔφη, εἴρηκας.

Ἔστιν δέ γε, ἔφην, φρόνιμός τε καὶ ἀγαθὸς ὁ ἄδικος, ὁ δὲ δίκαιος οὐδέτερα ;

Καὶ τοῦτ', ἔφη, εὖ. 5

Οὐκοῦν, ἦν δ' ἐγώ, καὶ ἔοικε τῷ φρονίμῳ καὶ τῷ ἀγαθῷ ὁ ἄδικος, ὁ δὲ δίκαιος οὐκ ἔοικεν ;

Πῶς γὰρ οὐ μέλλει, ἔφη, ὁ τοιοῦτος ὢν καὶ ἐοικέναι τοῖς τοιούτοις, ὁ δὲ μὴ ἐοικέναι ;

Καλῶς. τοιοῦτος ἄρα ἐστὶν ἑκάτερος αὐτῶν οἷσπερ 10 ἔοικεν ;

Ἀλλὰ τί μέλλει ; ἔφη.

Εἶεν, ὦ Θρασύμαχε· μουσικὸν δέ τινα λέγεις, e ἕτερον δὲ ἄμουσον ;

Ἔγωγε.

Πότερον φρόνιμον καὶ πότερον ἄφρονα ;

Τὸν μὲν μουσικὸν δήπου φρόνιμον, τὸν δὲ ἄμουσον 5 ἄφρονα.

Οὐκοῦν καὶ ἅπερ φρόνιμον, ἀγαθόν, ἃ δὲ ἄφρονα, κακόν ;

Ναί.

Τί δὲ ἰατρικόν ; οὐχ οὕτως ; 10

Οὕτως.

Δοκεῖ ἂν οὖν τίς σοι, ὦ ἄριστε, μουσικὸς ἀνὴρ ἁρμοττόμενος λύραν ἐθέλειν μουσικοῦ ἀνδρὸς ἐν τῇ ἐπιτάσει καὶ ἀνέσει τῶν χορδῶν πλεονεκτεῖν ἢ ἀξιοῦν πλέον ἔχειν ; 15

Οὐκ ἔμοιγε.

Τί δέ ; ἀμούσου ;

Ἀνάγκη, ἔφη.

Τί δὲ ἰατρικός ; ἐν τῇ ἐδωδῇ ἢ πόσει ἐθέλειν ἄν 350 τι ἰατρικοῦ πλεονεκτεῖν ἢ ἀνδρὸς ἢ πράγματος ;

Οὐ δῆτα.

Μὴ ἰατρικοῦ δέ ;

5   Ναί.

Περὶ πάσης δὴ ὅρα ἐπιστήμης τε καὶ ἀνεπιστη-
μοσύνης εἴ τίς σοι δοκεῖ ἐπιστήμων ὁστισοῦν πλείω
ἂν ἐθέλειν αἱρεῖσθαι ἢ ὅσα ἄλλος ἐπιστήμων ἢ πράττειν
ἢ λέγειν, καὶ οὐ ταὐτὰ τῷ ὁμοίῳ ἑαυτῷ εἰς τὴν αὐτὴν
10 πρᾶξιν.

'Αλλ' ἴσως, ἔφη, ἀνάγκη τοῦτό γε οὕτως ἔχειν.

Τί δὲ ὁ ἀνεπιστήμων ; οὐχὶ ὁμοίως μὲν ἐπιστήμονος
b πλεονεκτήσειεν ἄν, ὁμοίως δὲ ἀνεπιστήμονος ;

῎Ισως.

'Ο δὲ ἐπιστήμων σοφός ;

Φημί.

5   'Ο δὲ σοφὸς ἀγαθός ;

Φημί.

'Ο ἄρα ἀγαθός τε καὶ σοφὸς τοῦ μὲν ὁμοίου
οὐκ ἐθελήσει πλεονεκτεῖν, τοῦ δὲ ἀνομοίου τε καὶ
ἐναντίου.

10   ῎Εοικεν, ἔφη.

'Ο δὲ κακός τε καὶ ἀμαθὴς τοῦ τε ὁμοίου καὶ τοῦ
ἐναντίου.

Φαίνεται.

Οὐκοῦν, ὦ Θρασύμαχε, ἦν δ' ἐγώ, ὁ ἄδικος ἡμῖν
15 τοῦ ἀνομοίου τε καὶ ὁμοίου πλεονεκτεῖ ; ἢ οὐχ οὕτως
ἔλεγες ;

῎Εγωγε, ἔφη.

c   'Ο δέ γε δίκαιος τοῦ μὲν ὁμοίου οὐ πλεονεκτήσει,
τοῦ δὲ ἀνομοίου ;

Ναί.

῎Εοικεν ἄρα, ἦν δ' ἐγώ, ὁ μὲν δίκαιος τῷ σοφῷ
5 καὶ ἀγαθῷ, ὁ δὲ ἄδικος τῷ κακῷ καὶ ἀμαθεῖ.

Κινδυνεύει.

Ἀλλὰ μὴν ὡμολογοῦμεν, ᾧ γε ὅμοιος ἑκάτερος εἴη,
τοιοῦτον καὶ ἑκάτερον εἶναι.

Ὡμολογοῦμεν γάρ.

Ὁ μὲν ἄρα δίκαιος ἡμῖν ἀναπέφανται ὧν ἀγαθός 10
τε καὶ σοφός, ὁ δὲ ἄδικος ἀμαθής τε καὶ κακύς.

Ὁ δὴ Θρασύμαχος ὡμολόγησε μὲν πάντα ταῦτα,
οὐχ ὡς ἐγὼ νῦν ῥᾳδίως λέγω, ἀλλ' ἑλκόμενος καὶ d
μόγις, μετὰ ἱδρῶτος θαυμαστοῦ ὅσου, ἅτε καὶ θέρους
ὄντος· τότε καὶ εἶδον ἐγώ, πρότερον δὲ οὔπω, Θρασύμαχον ἐρυθριῶντα· ἐπειδὴ δὲ οὖν διωμολογησάμεθα
τὴν δικαιοσύνην ἀρετὴν εἶναι καὶ σοφίαν, τὴν δὲ 5
ἀδικίαν κακίαν τε καὶ ἀμαθίαν, Εἶεν, ἦν δ' ἐγώ, τοῦτο
μὲν ἡμῖν οὕτω κείσθω, ἔφαμεν δὲ δὴ καὶ ἰσχυρὸν
εἶναι τὴν ἀδικίαν. ἢ οὐ μέμνησαι, ὦ Θρασύμαχε;

Μέμνημαι, ἔφη· ἀλλ' ἔμοιγε οὐδὲ ἃ νῦν λέγεις
ἀρέσκει, καὶ ἔχω περὶ αὐτῶν λέγειν. εἰ οὖν λέγοιμι, 10
εὖ οἶδ' ὅτι δημηγορεῖν ἄν με φαίης. ἢ οὖν ἔα με e
εἰπεῖν ὅσα βούλομαι, ἤ, εἰ βούλει ἐρωτᾶν, ἐρώτα·
ἐγὼ δέ σοι, ὥσπερ ταῖς γραυσὶν ταῖς τοὺς μύθους
λεγούσαις, " εἶεν " ἐρῶ καὶ κατανεύσομαι καὶ ἀνανεύσομαι. 5

Μηδαμῶς, ἦν δ' ἐγώ, παρά γε τὴν σαυτοῦ δόξαν.

Ὥστε σοί, ἔφη, ἀρέσκειν, ἐπειδήπερ οὐκ ἐᾷς λέγειν.
καίτοι τί ἄλλο βούλει;

Οὐδὲν μὰ Δία, ἦν δ' ἐγώ, ἀλλ' εἴπερ τοῦτο ποιήσεις,
ποίει· ἐγὼ δὲ ἐρωτήσω. 10

Ἐρώτα δή.

Τοῦτο τοίνυν ἐρωτῶ, ὅπερ ἄρτι, ἵνα καὶ ἐξῆς
διασκεψώμεθα τὸν λόγον, ὁποῖόν τι τυγχάνει ὂν 351
δικαιοσύνη πρὸς ἀδικίαν. ἐλέχθη γάρ που ὅτι καὶ
δυνατώτερον καὶ ἰσχυρότερον εἴη ἀδικία δικαιοσύνης·
νῦν δὲ γ', ἔφην, εἴπερ σοφία τε καὶ ἀρετή ἐστιν δικαιοσύνη,

5 ῥᾳδίως οἶμαι φανήσεται καὶ ἰσχυρότερον ἀδικίας,
ἐπειδήπερ ἐστὶν ἀμαθία ἡ ἀδικία—οὐδεὶς ἂν ἔτι τοῦτο
ἀγνοήσειεν—ἀλλ᾽ οὔ τι οὕτως ἁπλῶς, ὦ Θρασύμαχε,
ἔγωγε ἐπιθυμῶ, ἀλλὰ τῇδέ πη σκέψασθαι· πόλιν
b φαίης ἂν ἄδικον εἶναι καὶ ἄλλας πόλεις ἐπιχειρεῖν
δουλοῦσθαι ἀδίκως καὶ καταδεδουλῶσθαι, πολλὰς δὲ
καὶ ὑφ᾽ ἑαυτῇ ἔχειν δουλωσαμένην ;

Πῶς γὰρ οὔκ ; ἔφη. καὶ τοῦτό γε ἡ ἀρίστη μάλιστα
5 ποιήσει καὶ τελεώτατα οὖσα ἄδικος.

Μανθάνω, ἔφην, ὅτι σὸς οὗτος ἦν ὁ λόγος. ἀλλὰ
τόδε περὶ αὐτοῦ σκοπῶ· πότερον ἡ κρείττων γιγνομένη
πόλις πόλεως ἄνευ δικαιοσύνης τὴν δύναμιν ταύτην
ἕξει, ἢ ἀνάγκη αὐτῇ μετὰ δικαιοσύνης ;

c Εἰ μέν, ἔφη, ὡς σὺ ἄρτι ἔλεγες ἔχει—ἡ δικαιοσύνη
σοφία—μετὰ δικαιοσύνης· εἰ δ᾽ ὡς ἐγὼ ἔλεγον, μετὰ
ἀδικίας.

Πάνυ ἄγαμαι, ἦν δ᾽ ἐγώ, ὦ Θρασύμαχε, ὅτι οὐκ
5 ἐπινεύεις μόνον καὶ ἀνανεύεις, ἀλλὰ καὶ ἀποκρίνῃ
πάνυ καλῶς.

Σοὶ γάρ, ἔφη, χαρίζομαι.

Εὖ γε σὺ ποιῶν· ἀλλὰ δὴ καὶ τόδε μοι χάρισαι
καὶ λέγε· δοκεῖς ἂν ἢ πόλιν ἢ στρατόπεδον ἢ λῃστὰς
10 ἢ κλέπτας ἢ ἄλλο τι ἔθνος, ὅσα κοινῇ ἐπί τι ἔρχεται
ἀδίκως, πρᾶξαι ἄν τι δύνασθαι, εἰ ἀδικοῖεν ἀλλήλους ;
d Οὐ δῆτα, ἦ δ᾽ ὅς.

Τί δ᾽ εἰ μὴ ἀδικοῖεν ; οὐ μᾶλλον ;

Πάνυ γε.

Στάσεις γάρ που, ὦ Θρασύμαχε, ἥ γε ἀδικία καὶ
5 μίση καὶ μάχας ἐν ἀλλήλοις παρέχει, ἡ δὲ δικαιοσύνη
ὁμόνοιαν καὶ φιλίαν· ἦ γάρ ;

Ἔστω, ἦ δ᾽ ὅς, ἵνα σοι μὴ διαφέρωμαι.

Ἀλλ᾽ εὖ γε σὺ ποιῶν, ὦ ἄριστε. τόδε δέ μοι λέγε·

ἆρα εἰ τοῦτο ἔργον ἀδικίας, μῖσος ἐμποιεῖν ὅπου ἂν
ἐνῇ, οὐ καὶ ἐν ἐλευθέροις τε καὶ δούλοις ἐγγιγνομένη 10
μισεῖν ποιήσει ἀλλήλους καὶ στασιάζειν καὶ ἀδυνάτους
εἶναι κοινῇ μετ' ἀλλήλων πράττειν ;   e
    Πάνυ γε.
    Τί δὲ ἂν ἐν δυοῖν ἐγγένηται ; οὐ διοίσονται καὶ
μισήσουσιν καὶ ἐχθροὶ ἔσονται ἀλλήλοις τε καὶ τοῖς
δικαίοις ;   5
    Ἔσονται, ἔφη.
    Ἐὰν δὲ δή, ὦ θαυμάσιε, ἐν ἑνὶ ἐγγένηται ἀδικία,
μῶν μὴ ἀπολεῖ τὴν αὐτῆς δύναμιν, ἢ οὐδὲν ἧττον
ἕξει ;
    Μηδὲν ἧττον ἐχέτω, ἔφη.   10
    Οὐκοῦν τοιάνδε τινὰ φαίνεται ἔχουσα τὴν δύναμιν,
οἵαν, ᾧ ἂν ἐγγένηται, εἴτε πόλει τινὶ εἴτε γένει εἴτε
στρατοπέδῳ εἴτε ἄλλῳ ὁτῳοῦν, πρῶτον μὲν ἀδύνατον 352
αὐτὸ ποιεῖν πράττειν μεθ' αὑτοῦ διὰ τὸ στασιάζειν
καὶ διαφέρεσθαι, ἔτι δ' ἐχθρὸν εἶναι ἑαυτῷ τε καὶ
τῷ ἐναντίῳ παντὶ καὶ τῷ δικαίῳ ; οὐχ οὕτως ;
    Πάνυ γε.   5
    Καὶ ἐν ἑνὶ δὴ οἶμαι ἐνοῦσα ταῦτα ταῦτα ποιήσει
ἅπερ πέφυκεν ἐργάζεσθαι· πρῶτον μὲν ἀδύνατον
αὐτὸν πράττειν ποιήσει στασιάζοντα καὶ οὐχ ὁμονοοῦντα
αὐτὸν ἑαυτῷ, ἔπειτα ἐχθρὸν καὶ ἑαυτῷ καὶ τοῖς δικαίοις·
ἦ γάρ ;   10
    Ναί.
    Δίκαιοι δέ γ' εἰσίν, ὦ φίλε, καὶ οἱ θεοι ;
    Ἔστων, ἔφη.
    Καὶ θεοῖς ἄρα ἐχθρὸς ἔσται ὁ ἄδικος, ὦ Θρασύμαχε, b
ὁ δὲ δίκαιος φίλος.
    Εὐωχοῦ τοῦ λόγου, ἔφη, θαρρων· οὐ γὰρ ἔγωγέ
σοι ἐναντιώσομαι, ἵνα μὴ τοῖσδε ἀπέχθωμαι.

5 Ἴθι δή, ἦν δ' ἐγώ, καὶ τὰ λοιπά μοι τῆς ἑστιάσεως
ἀποπλήρωσον ἀποκρινόμενος ὥσπερ καὶ νῦν. ὅτι μὲν
γὰρ καὶ σοφώτεροι καὶ ἀμείνους καὶ δυνατώτεροι
πράττειν οἱ δίκαιοι φαίνονται, οἱ δὲ ἄδικοι οὐδὲ πράττειν
c μετ' ἀλλήλων οἷοί τε, ἀλλὰ δὴ καὶ οὕς φαμεν ἐρρωμένως
πώποτέ τι μετ' ἀλλήλων κοινῇ πρᾶξαι ἀδίκους ὄντας,
τοῦτο οὐ παντάπασιν ἀληθὲς λέγομεν· οὐ γὰρ ἂν
ἀπείχοντο ἀλλήλων κομιδῇ ὄντες ἄδικοι, ἀλλὰ δῆλον
5 ὅτι ἐνῆν τις αὐτοῖς δικαιοσύνη, ἣ αὐτοὺς ἐποίει μήτοι
καὶ ἀλλήλους γε καὶ ἐφ' οὓς ᾖσαν ἅμα ἀδικεῖν, δι'
ἣν ἔπραξαν ἃ ἔπραξαν, ὥρμησαν δὲ ἐπὶ τὰ ἄδικα
ἀδικίᾳ ἡμιμόχθηροι ὄντες, ἐπεὶ οἵ γε παμπόνηροι
καὶ τελέως ἄδικοι τελέως εἰσὶ καὶ πράττειν ἀδύνατοι·
d ταῦτα μὲν οὖν ὅτι οὕτως ἔχει μανθάνω, ἀλλ' οὐχ ὡς
σὺ τὸ πρῶτον ἐτίθεσο· εἰ δὲ καὶ ἄμεινον ζῶσιν οἱ
δίκαιοι τῶν ἀδίκων καὶ εὐδαιμονέστεροί εἰσιν, ὅπερ
τὸ ὕστερον προυθέμεθα σκέψασθαι, σκεπτέον. φαίνονται
5 μὲν οὖν καὶ νῦν, ὥς γέ μοι δοκεῖ, ἐξ ὧν εἰρήκαμεν·
ὅμως δ' ἔτι βέλτιον σκεπτέον. οὐ γὰρ περὶ τοῦ
ἐπιτυχόντος ὁ λόγος, ἀλλὰ περὶ τοῦ ὄντινα τρόπον
χρὴ ζῆν.

Σκόπει δή, ἔφη.

10 Σκοπῶ, ἦν δ' ἐγώ. καί μοι λέγε· δοκεῖ τί σοι
εἶναι ἵππου ἔργον ;

e Ἔμοιγε.

Ἆρ' οὖν τοῦτο ἂν θείης καὶ ἵππου καὶ ἄλλου
ὁτουοῦν ἔργον, ὃ ἂν ἢ μόνῳ ἐκείνῳ ποιῇ τις ἢ ἄριστα ;

Οὐ μανθάνω, ἔφη.

5 Ἀλλ' ὧδε· ἔσθ' ὅτῳ ἂν ἄλλῳ ἴδοις ἢ ὀφθαλμοῖς ;

Οὐ δῆτα.

Τί δέ ; ἀκούσαις ἄλλῳ ἢ ὠσίν ;

Οὐδαμῶς.

Οὐκοῦν δικαίως [ἂν] ταῦτα τούτων φαμὲν ἔργα εἶναι ;

Πάνυ γε. 10

Τί δέ ; μαχαίρᾳ ἂν ἀμπέλου κλῆμα ἀποτέμοις καὶ 353
σμίλῃ καὶ ἄλλοις πολλοῖς ;

Πῶς γὰρ οὔ ;

'Αλλ' οὐδενί γ' ἂν οἶμαι οὕτω καλῶς ὡς δρεπάνῳ
τῷ ἐπὶ τούτῳ ἐργασθέντι. 5

'Αληθῆ.

*Αρ' οὖν οὐ τοῦτο τούτου ἔργον θήσομεν ;

Θήσομεν μὲν οὖν.

Νῦν δὴ οἶμαι ἄμεινον ἂν μάθοις ὃ ἄρτι ἠρώτων
πυνθανόμενος, εἰ οὐ τοῦτο ἑκάστου εἴη ἔργον ὃ ἂν ἢ 10
μόνον τι ἢ κάλλιστα τῶν ἄλλων ἀπεργάζηται.

'Αλλά, ἔφη, μανθάνω τε καί μοι δοκεῖ τοῦτο ἑκάστου
πράγματος ἔργον εἶναι. b

Εἶεν, ἦν δ' ἐγώ. οὐκοῦν καὶ ἀρετὴ δοκεῖ σοι εἶναι
ἑκάστῳ ᾧπερ καὶ ἔργον τι προστέτακται ; ἴωμεν δὲ
ἐπὶ τὰ αὐτὰ πάλιν· ὀφθαλμῶν, φαμέν, ἔστι τι ἔργον ;

*Εστιν. 5

*Αρ' οὖν καὶ ἀρετὴ ὀφθαλμῶν ἔστιν ;

Καὶ ἀρετή.

Τί δέ ; ὤτων ἦν τι ἔργον ;

Ναί.

Οὐκοῦν καὶ ἀρετή ; 10

Καὶ ἀρετή.

Τί δὲ πάντων πέρι τῶν ἄλλων ; οὐχ οὕτω ;

Οὕτω.

*Εχε δή· ἆρ' ἄν ποτε ὄμματα τὸ αὑτῶν ἔργον
καλῶς ἀπεργάσαιντο μὴ ἔχοντα τὴν αὑτῶν οἰκείαν c
ἀρετήν, ἀλλ' ἀντὶ τῆς ἀρετῆς κακίαν ;

Καὶ πῶς ἄν ; ἔφη· τυφλότητα γὰρ ἴσως λέγεις
ἀντὶ τῆς ὄψεως.

5 Ἥτις, ἦν δ᾽ ἐγώ, αὐτῶν ἡ ἀρετή· οὐ γάρ πω τοῦτο
ἐρωτῶ, ἀλλ᾽ εἰ τῇ οἰκείᾳ μὲν ἀρετῇ τὸ αὐτῶν ἔργον
εὖ ἐργάσεται τὰ ἐργαζόμενα, κακίᾳ δὲ κακῶς.

Ἀληθές, ἔφη, τοῦτό γε λέγεις.

Οὐκοῦν καὶ ὦτα στερόμενα τῆς αὐτῶν ἀρετῆς
10 κακῶς τὸ αὐτῶν ἔργον ἀπεργάσεται :

Πάνυ γε.

d Τίθεμεν οὖν καὶ τἆλλα πάντα εἰς τὸν αὐτὸν λόγον ;
Ἔμοιγε δοκεῖ.

Ἴθι δή, μετὰ ταῦτα τόδε σκέψαι. ψυχῆς ἔστιν τι
ἔργον ὃ ἄλλῳ τῶν ὄντων οὐδ᾽ ἂν ἑνὶ πράξαις, οἷον
5 τὸ τοιόνδε· τὸ ἐπιμελεῖσθαι καὶ ἄρχειν καὶ βουλεύεσθαι
καὶ τὰ τοιαῦτα πάντα, ἔσθ᾽ ὅτῳ ἄλλῳ ἢ ψυχῇ
δικαίως ἂν αὐτὰ ἀποδοῖμεν καὶ φαῖμεν ἴδια ἐκείνης
εἶναι ;

Οὐδενὶ ἄλλῳ.

10 Τί δ᾽ αὖ τὸ ζῆν ; οὐ ψυχῆς φήσομεν ἔργον εἶναι ;
Μάλιστά γ᾽, ἔφη.

Οὐκοῦν καὶ ἀρετήν φαμέν τινα ψυχῆς εἶναι ;
Φαμέν.

e Ἆρ᾽ οὖν ποτε, ὦ Θρασύμαχε, ψυχὴ τὰ αὑτῆς
ἔργα εὖ ἀπεργάσεται στερομένη τῆς οἰκείας ἀρετῆς,
ἢ ἀδύνατον ;
Ἀδύνατον.

5 Ἀνάγκη ἄρα κακῇ ψυχῇ κακῶς ἄρχειν καὶ ἐπιμελεῖσθαι, τῇ δὲ ἀγαθῇ πάντα ταῦτα εὖ πράττειν.
Ἀνάγκη.

Οὐκοῦν ἀρετήν γε συνεχωρήσαμεν ψυχῆς εἶναι
δικαιοσύνην, κακίαν δὲ ἀδικίαν ;

10 Συνεχωρήσαμεν γάρ.

Ἡ μὲν ἄρα δικαία ψυχὴ καὶ ὁ δίκαιος ἀνὴρ εὖ
βιώσεται, κακῶς δὲ ὁ ἄδικος.

Φαίνεται, ἔφη, κατὰ τὸν σὸν λόγον.

'Αλλὰ μὴν ὅ γε εὖ ζῶν μακάριός τε καὶ εὐδαίμων, **354**
ὁ δὲ μὴ τἀναντία.

Πῶς γὰρ οὔ ;

'Ο μὲν δίκαιος ἄρα εὐδαίμων, ὁ δ' ἄδικος ἄθλιος.

῎Εστων, ἔφη. 5

'Αλλὰ μὴν ἄθλιόν γε εἶναι οὐ λυσιτελεῖ, εὐδαίμονα
δέ.

Πῶς γὰρ οὔ ;

Οὐδέποτ' ἄρα, ὦ μακάριε Θρασύμαχε, λυσιτελέστερον
ἀδικία δικαιοσύνης. 10

Ταῦτα δή σοι, ἔφη, ὦ Σώκρατες, εἱστιάσθω ἐν τοῖς
Βενδιδίοις.

'Υπὸ σοῦ γε, ἦν δ' ἐγώ, ὦ Θρασύμαχε, ἐπειδή μοι
πρᾷος ἐγένου καὶ χαλεπαίνων ἐπαύσω. οὐ μέντοι
καλῶς γε εἱστίαμαι, δι' ἐμαυτὸν ἀλλ' οὐ διὰ σέ· ἀλλ' **b**
ὥσπερ οἱ λίχνοι τοῦ ἀεὶ παραφερομένου ἀπογεύονται
ἁρπάζοντες, πρὶν τοῦ προτέρου μετρίως ἀπολαῦσαι,
καὶ ἐγώ μοι δοκῶ οὕτω, πρὶν ὃ τὸ πρῶτον ἐσκοποῦμεν
εὑρεῖν, τὸ δίκαιον ὅτι ποτ' ἐστίν, ἀφέμενος ἐκείνου 5
ὁρμῆσαι ἐπὶ τὸ σκέψασθαι περὶ αὐτοῦ εἴτε κακία
ἐστὶν καὶ ἀμαθία, εἴτε σοφία καὶ ἀρετή, καὶ ἐμπεσόντος
αὖ ὕστερον λόγου, ὅτι λυσιτελέστερον ἡ ἀδικία τῆς
δικαιοσύνης, οὐκ ἀπεσχόμην τὸ μὴ οὐκ ἐπὶ τοῦτο
ἐλθεῖν ἀπ' ἐκείνου, ὥστε μοι νυνὶ γέγονεν ἐκ τοῦ 10
διαλόγου μηδὲν εἰδέναι· ὁπότε γὰρ τὸ δίκαιον μὴ **c**
οἶδα ὅ ἐστιν, σχολῇ εἴσομαι εἴτε ἀρετή τις οὖσα τυγχάνει
εἴτε καὶ οὔ, καὶ πότερον ὁ ἔχων αὐτὸ οὐκ εὐδαίμων
ἐστὶν ἢ εὐδαίμων.

NOTES

327 a 1 Κατέβην ... ἄγοντες. This opening sentence is the subject of a famous anecdote. It was related—by authorities living in the second century B.C., Euphorion and Panaetius—that among papers left by Plato was found one containing these opening words written in various orders (Diogenes Laertius, iii, 1, 37). Critics have interpreted the story according to their own taste : thus Dionysius of Halicarnassus, an expert on style, wonders at the fact that Plato, though now eighty years old, was still ' combing and curling ' his Dialogues : whereas Wilamowitz (*Platon*, ii, 257) approaches the story in a strictly rational way—suggesting that Plato may have started to rewrite the *Republic* in order to combine it with the *Timaeus*.

From the fact that the paper was found, it does not follow that it had been recently written. If the story is true at all, it is likely that the paper was a manuscript of the *Republic*. There is no evidence that Plato ever made a ' second edition ' of any Dialogue, and he was composing fresh works until the day of his death.

— Πειραιᾶ : the distance from Athens to the Piraeus is about five miles. The circumflex accent on the last syllable of the Greek name indicates a contraction from -εα. Πειραιεύς was, as Tucker points out, originally an adjective qualifying λιμήν, ' the Piraean harbour '.

a 2 τῇ θεῷ : Socrates, then, goes to the Piraeus in order to pray to the goddess, and to see how the festival will be organized on its first introduction. From Book I, 354 a, the festival is seen to be that of Bendis, a Thracian goddess sometimes identified by the Greeks with Artemis. Later there were temples of Artemis and Bendis standing together on the promontory of Munichia (Xenophon, *Hellenica*, ii, 4, 11, writing of events in 400 B.C.). As the festival is certainly that of Bendis, it is probable that she is also the goddess understood in τῇ θεῷ, though it is rather strange that Socrates should decide to pray to a goddess with whom he is not yet acquainted.

'Η θεός, to an Athenian speaking in his own country, would normally mean Athena : cf. *Tim.* 21a, 26e ; but this does not suit the context here. Another goddess who has a claim to be considered is Artemis ; she had a temple at the Piraeus in a prominent position, and may well have been its patron. As Bendis was alleged to be identical with Artemis, her introduction might be made to coincide with some regular festival of Artemis, and on such an occasion the prayer of Socrates would be natural. This theory would, moreover, explain the statement that there were *two* processions, one by the Thracians, and one by the ' natives ', i.e. dwellers at the Piraeus, ἐπιχώριοι (see below).

In a comedy produced in 444 B.C., the *Thracian Women*, the poet

78

Cratinus introduced worshippers of Bendis. The name, and some characteristics of the cult, were therefore known by the middle of the fifth century ; and Βένδις has been restored with some plausibility in an inscription, I.G. i, 210, p. 93. But this is no reason why the official introduction of the goddess should not have come some years later. Plato's evidence on this point, if it were more definite, would be decisive ; as it is we must be content with the conjecture that the dramatic date of the *Republic* is at about the time of the Peace of Nicias (see p. 20). The god Asclepius, to whom Socrates owed an offering at the time of his death, had been likewise introduced from Epidaurus to Athens with a formal ceremony in 420 B.C.

Thrace was the home of the cults of Dionysus and Orpheus, and in general of the belief in the immortality or transmigration of the soul. Perhaps this was the reason why Bendis also was a favourite with the Athenians.

Proclus records that in his day (fifth century A.D.) the festival of Bendis fell on the 19th of Thargelion, i.e. early in June : *cf.* 350d ἅτε καὶ θέρους ὄντος.

a 5 πομπή, procession : hence the idea of show or solemnity, which survives in the English ' pomp '.

Πέμπειν, in its original meaning, is not simply ' to send ', but ' to escort ' ; and the πομπή is an official send-off, such as Odysseus receives from the Phaeacians. Since Homer's time the two meanings ' to send ' and ' to escort in a procession ' have fallen apart. Translate ' the procession displayed by the Thracians '. *Ἣν* is cognate accusative.

a 6 Θρᾷκες : ' Probably resident aliens living for commercial purposes in the Piraeus, which at all times contained a large admixture of foreign population ' (Adam). Others have supposed that οἱ Θρᾷκες refers to a special delegation from Thrace—taking ἔπεμπον in its accustomed sense.

b 1 πρὸς τὸ ἄστυ, ' to town ', i.e. Athens, as distinct from the Piraeus.

— κατιδών, ' observing ', ' noticing '—not quite the same as ἰδών.

b 3 ἑ, ' himself ', Latin *se*. This was undoubtedly an old form, but in later Attic literature it is almost confined to Plato. Perhaps it had survived in conversation.

b 4 μου . . . λαβόμενος τοῦ ἱματίου, ' grasping me by my cloak '. Both genitives are partitive, but one is a degree more definite than the other.

b 6, 7 αὐτός . . . Οὗτος. More conversational idioms.

(1) Αὐτός = ' his master ', an expression used of any kind of superior —a parent, a teacher, etc. Cf. Aristoph. *Clouds*, 218 :

Φέρε τις γὰρ οὗτος οὑπὶ τῆς κρεμάθρας ἀνήρ ;
Αὐτός. Τίς αὐτός ; Σωκράτης.

(2) Οὗτος, ' here he is,'—grammarians describe this as the ' deictic ' use.

b 7 Ἀλλὰ περιμένετε. Ἀλλὰ περιμενοῦμεν. This repetition must have occurred frequently in conversation ; ἀλλά is often used in making a request, and no less often in granting one (cf. *mais certainement*).

Notice that the Greek for ' to wait *for* ' is the compound περιμένειν ; μένειν is generally intransitive. The former corresponds to the Latin *exspectare*.

b 8 ἦ δ' ὅς. 'The whole expression ἦ δ' ὅς is archaic. The verb ἠμί is found in Attic Greek only in the survivals ἦν and ἦ , and then only in conjunction with δ'ἐγώ and δ' ὅς respectively.' (Tucker) : ὅς is the old demonstrative pronoun, ' he '.

c 3 ὡς ἀπό : Two slightly different interpretations of ὡς are possible : (1) ' as though ', ' apparently '. (2) ' as they naturally would.' Probably the former is intended.

c 11 ἔτι ἓν λείπεται. This reading is greatly preferable in sense to the ἔτι ἐλλείπεται of the best manuscripts, which some editors retain. In the earliest stage of the transmission of the text, ἐλλείπεται would be written ΕΝΛΕΙΠΕΤΑΙ.

The phrase τὸ . . . ἀφεῖναι serves here as a noun : ' the possibility that we may persuade you . . .'

ἀφιέναι has two main meanings : (1) to discharge, as of a weapon, (2) to dismiss, set free. (It is really a difference of degree : we ' throw ' something which has no natural impetus : we ' release ' something which has one.)

c 13, 15 μὴ ἀκούοντας . . . μὴ ἀκουσομένων. Μή is natural in the first case, because the meaning is conditional, ' if we refuse to listen.' In the second case, it is required because the main verb διανοεῖσθε is in the imperative.

Ὡς ἀκουσομένων sc. ἡμῶν genitive absolute.

328 a 2 λαμπάς, ' torch-race.' It was a relay race in which the torch was handed from one runner to another, and had to be kept burning ; Herodotus, viii, 98 mentions one held in honour of Hephaestus. Cf. *Laws*, 776 b, καθάπερ λαμπάδα τὸν βίον παραδιδόντας ἄλλοις ἐξ ἄλλων : Lucretius, ii, 79, et quasi cursores vitai lampada tradunt. Notice also λαμπάδια for ' torches ' ; this is not because there is any special need for a diminutive, but because λαμπάς has just been used in a different sense.

a 6 καὶ πρός γε : πρός in this expression is adverbial, ' besides '.

— ἐξαναστησόμεθα : neither the supper nor the spectacle which was to follow it are again mentioned. This might be held to support the view that Plato originally planned the scene of Book I by itself.

a 9 αὐτόθι, i.e. without returning to the city : this implies that such a συνουσία anywhere but in Athens was a comparative rarity.

a 10 μὴ ἄλλως ποιεῖτε : an affirmative request is often reinforced in this way (cf. 328 d, 338 a).

b 3 οἴκαδε εἰς τοῦ Πολεμάρχου : ' to the house of Polemarchus.'

This could be said without implying that P. was, as yet, the master of the house. Cephalus, when he invites Socrates to visit them more often, seems to speak in that capacity ; and it certainly appears that he has not yet left his fortune, or part of it, to his sons (330 *b*). Polemarchus, as the eldest son, is his heir (331 *d*).

Probably all three brothers are still living in a house owned by their father ; and Lysias, already a student of rhetoric, has brought Thrasymachus as his guest. It appears from his speech against Eratosthenes (12, 8 and 12, 16) that in 404 B.C. Lysias lived in his own house in the Piraeus ; and Polemarchus either at Athens or elsewhere in the Piraeus. But this was long after the present scene.

b 5 καὶ δὴ καί : this suggests both that he was a rare visitor, and that he was an important one.

b 6 Καλχηδόνιον : ' The proper name of the town, as given on its coins was Καλχηδών.' (Tucker : he quotes evidence that the spelling Χαλχηδών also existed in the fifth century, and was due to a 'cockneyism' in the Attic speech, which tended to bring in too many aspirates.)

c 1 καί emphasizes the whole sentence, not ἑωράκη alone : ' for indeed it was a long time since I had seen him,' not ' it was long since I had even seen him '. διά with the genitive has the sense of *traversing*, so that διά χρόνου literally means, ' I had passed through a long time since . . .'

c 2 καθῆστο . . . αὐλῇ. Cephalus sits ' on a kind of cushioned chair ' ; he still has the wreath (στέφανος) which he had worn for the sacrifice in the court. The sacrifice had no connection with the festival ; it was a sacrifice to Zeus Ἑρκεῖος, Zeus as the protector of the household. There is no special point in the cushioned chair, unless it is that Plato is describing a scene which he really remembered.

c 6 ἠσπάζετο : the imperfect tense shows that he *began* his welcome as soon as he saw Socrates : it is followed by an aorist, εἶπεν.

c 7 οὐδὲ θαμίζεις requires explanation. Either the right reading is οὐδέ, as in the Paris ms. ; and in this case οὐδέ must *somehow* have its proper sense of ' not even ' ; or we may emend to οὐ δέ, οὐ δή, or οὔ τι.

(1) If οὐδέ is right, the phrase means ' You are not a frequent visitor *either*,' and it is implied that Cephalus could charge Socrates with other lapses which he does not mention.

(Cf. the American idiom, ' it is *too* ', ' I will *too* '.) Tucker is right in saying that οὐδέ, if correct, must be regarded as one of those colloquial idioms which, logical enough in their origin, imperceptibly shift their application until they defy strict analysis.

(2) οὐ δή would mean ' you are certainly not a frequent visitor '. Jowett and Campbell recommend οὐ δέ, saying that δέ is adversative to the idea contained in ἠσπάζετο, ' you are welcome, but . . .' These two suggestions do not carry conviction, and I am far more inclined

to read οὔ τι. Cephalus would then be quoting from Homer. Calypso says to Hermes (Od. v, 87) :

τίπτε μοι, Ἑρμεία χρυσόρραπι, εἰλήλουθας

αἰδοῖός τε φίλος τε ; πάρος γε μὲν οὔ τι θαμίζεις.

(Cf. also Il. xviii, 386.) Cephalus is fond of quotation, and the whole scene here is slightly Homeric.

328 d 1   ἡμεῖς, i.e. both Cephalus and his sons.

— ὡς εὖ ἴσθι ὅτι, 'since you may be sure that.'

d 8   Καὶ μήν : the force of this is, 'I can entirely agree, for it is a pleasure to me . . .'

e 4   τραχεῖα :   Tucker notes that Plato not seldom omits πότερον in a pair of questions in indirect speech ; he quotes Theait. 161 d, τὴν δόξαν κυριώτερος ἔσται ἐπισκέψασθαι ἕτερος τὴν ἑτέρου, ὀρθὴ ἢ ψευδής

e 5   ὃ τί σοι φαίνεται τοῦτο :   I prefer here the view of Jowett and Campbell : τοῦτο is the question which Socrates has mentioned, and the phrase means 'what is your view of this question'.   It might be thought that τοῦτο was the antecedent of ὃ . . . εἶναι ;   this would not greatly affect the meaning, but it would be less natural, and would destroy the pleasant informality of the sentence.   Ἐνταῦθα is the real antecedent of ὃ.

e 6   ὃ . . . οἱ ποιηταί.   Two points are doubtful—the construction of εἶναι, and the meaning of ἐπὶ γήραος οὐδῷ.

(1) If εἶναι means 'exists ', ' is situated ', we have the translation ' you have reached that point in human life which lies, according to the poets, at the threshold of old age '.   The singular fact, however, is not that poets assert the existence of this period, but that they call it by a picturesque name.   So it is better to translate ' the period which the poets call " being at the threshold of old age " '.   εἶναι is virtually a noun.

(2) In Homer the phrase ἐπὶ γήραος οὐδῷ denotes *extreme* old age. How does it come to have this sense ?   ' The threshold of old age ' would suggest the *beginning* of the last phase of life.   Some scholars are inclined to believe that γήραος is descriptive of οὐδῷ ' old age, the threshold '—life being conceived as a house which we enter at birth and depart from at death.   But it is more natural to suppose that *old age* is the house, and that ἐπὶ γήραος οὐδῷ is ' at the *further extremity* of old age '.   Cf. our colloquialism ' with one foot in the grave '— for which the comedians, and Longus, the novelist, have the striking equivalent τυμβογέρων.

Dr. Leaf at one time maintained, in a note on Il. xxii, 60, that οὐδός in the Homeric phrase was ὁδός, ' the *path* of old age ' ; and the present passage, following close on a comparison of life to a journey (328 e 2), might seem to support his view.   But the use of ἐπί is in this case not entirely natural, and the metaphor of a threshold has more of the picturesque quality of a proverbial phrase.

e 7   χαλεπὸν τοῦ βίου, ' an unpleasant part of life,'—a partitive genitive.   The words πότερον . . . ἐξαγγέλλεις depend loosely on φαίνεται in l. 5 ; they make the question put to Cephalus somewhat more precise.

329 a 4 παροιμίαν : The proverb was ἧλιξ ἧλικα τέρπει (*Phaedrus*, 240 c.)

a 7 τῶν τοιούτων ἔχεται, 'which go along with these.' ἔχεσθαι is 'to cling to', hence 'follow' and—metaphorically—'belong to the same class'.

a 9 εὖ ζῶντες . . . οὐδὲ ζῶντες 'Once they used to live well, now they are not alive at all'. The first ζῶντες represents an imperfect indicative.

b 1 τὰς τῶν οἰκείων προπηλακίσεις τοῦ γήρως, 'the insults which an old man suffers from his relatives.' For the two genitives, one subjective and the other objective, cf. *Phaedrus*, 244 c : τήν γε τῶν ἐμφρόνων ζήτησιν τοῦ μέλλοντος.

b 2 ἐπὶ τούτῳ δὴ . . . αἴτιον, 'they make a song of all the sufferings which they have to endure from old age.' Notice the Greek construction, γῆρας occurring in the main clause.

δή has three distinct uses : (1) to indicate surprise and irony, 'indeed'; (2) to sum up an inference, 'therefore'; (3) to add emphasis to a statement, 'emphatically.' In this context the last sense is most appropriate, 'it is especially for this reason . . . .'

b 5 τὰ αὐτὰ ταῦτα ἐπεπόνθη, 'should have experienced the same feeling.' πέπονθα, though strictly the perfect of πάσχω, is almost equivalent to a verb in the present tense meaning 'feel'. Plato could not have said τὰ αὐτὰ ἂν ἔπασχον, which would mean 'I should have undergone the same treatment'.

b 6 ἕνεκά γε γήρως, 'as far as old age is concerned.'

b 8 Σοφοκλεῖ. Sophocles was said to have led a chorus of boys which celebrated the victory of Salamis in 480 B.C., so that he was in fact an old or oldish man at the supposed time of the Dialogue. See the Introduction.

It is interesting that Sophocles' reply to the questioner is εὐφημεῖ 'hush !', an expression used to deter people from words of ill omen. It would seem that though he claims to be free from the tyranny of the passions, he does not yet feel altogether immune.

c 8 ἐπειδὰν αἱ ἐπιθυμίαι παύσωνται κατατείνουσαι καὶ χαλάσωσιν, 'when passions cease to distract us, and relax their hold.' An object is understood with both verbs, viz. the man who is controlled by the emotions, especially pleasure and pain, as a puppet is by wires. (Cf. *Laws*, 644 e.) This explanation of the metaphor is due to Ast. Tucker's view that it is borrowed from torture on the rack is less probable. It is true that both verbs are also used intransitively by Plato and other writers (for κατατείνειν see 358 *d*, 367 *b*, 348 *a*), but it seems preferable to supply an object where possible.

d 1 δεσποτῶν . . . ἐστι . . . ἀπηλλάχθαι, ' one is delivered from a host of insane rulers ', *lit.* there is a deliverance. This is the ordinary predicative ἐστι, not ἔστι = is possible.

d 3 τῶν γε πρὸς τοὺς οἰκείους, i.e. the insults mentioned in 329 *b*, though the expression is now less definite. Πρός = in relation to.

e 8 λέγουσι μέν τι, ' they are partly right.'
λέγειν τι is to talk sense, opp. to οὐδὲν λέγειν, to talk nonsense.

— τὸ τοῦ Θεμιστοκλέους. Herodotus' version of this story (viii, 125) is slightly different, and perhaps nearer to the historical truth. The critic of Themistocles was Timodemus of Aphidnae, who, referring to the honours which he had received at Sparta, declared that he owed them to his having been born an Athenian. Themistocles retorted ' If I were from Belbina, it is true that I could not have become famous, but neither could you, if you were an Athenian '. Aphidnae was an Athenian deme, and Belbina a small island to the south of Sunium. Plato's version not only substitutes Seriphus for Belbina, but makes the critic a native of Seriphus. This is a barren little island which ' gained an evil notoriety in later classical days as a place of banishment for imperial victims ' (Warren).

330 a 4 ὁ ἐπιεικής. If Cephalus' statement were closely examined, much would depend on the meaning of this word. It has the same vagueness as ' respectable ' or ' decent ' would have in the mouth of some modern Cephalus. It is connected by derivation with εἴκειν, to make concessions.

a 6 ἑαυτῷ : a person must be at peace with himself before he can be a good friend to others.

a 7 ὧν = ἐκείνων ἅ.

b 1 Ποῖ' ἐπεκτησάμην ; ' How much more I have made ? ' The repeated question, with ποῖα, adds a note of surprise. Ποῖος ' implies a humorous feeling of contrast between the suggestion and the fact ' (Jowett and Campbell). More often it is definitely derisive or ironical. But perhaps the chief reason why Cephalus repeats the question is that he is rather deaf ; in any case it is a mannerism of old age, with no special point here.

b 4 πολλάκις τοσαύτης, ' many times as great '—the original sense of πολλάκις.

b 5 The conjecture Λυσίας is ingenious, in view of the name of Cephalus' own son ; but the name Λυσανίας is well known.

b 7 τούτοισιν ' The archaic dative in -οισι is tolerably often used by Plato ; in the *Republic* alone it recurs in 345 *e*, 388 *d*, 389 *b*, 468 *d* (Homer), 560 *e*, 564 *c*, 607 *b* (-αισι, poetic).' (*Adam*.) There may, however, be a special reason here : perhaps the form is (1) old-fashioned, and suitable to the age of Cephalus, or (2) provincial, and suitable to his Syracusan origin, or (3) playful and affectionate, ' these lads.'

b 9 οὗ τοι ἕνεκα ἠρόμην ' (This is) why I asked.' Cf. 491 *b* : ὃ μὲν πάντων θαυμαστότατον ἀκοῦσαι, ὅτι . . .

c 1 ὡς τὸ πολύ, ' for the most part.'

c 3 διπλῆ ᾗ οἱ ἄλλοι. ' The ἦ is like ἦ after διπλάσιος, πολλαπλάσιος, etc.' (*Adam*) The sentiment recurs in Aristotle, *Nic. Eth.*, 1120 *b* 14 : ἐλευθεριώτεροι δ' εἶναι δοκοῦσιν οἱ μὴ κτησάμενοι ἀλλὰ παραλαβόντες τὴν οὐσίαν, ἄπειροί τε γὰρ τῆς ἐνδείας, καὶ πάντες ἀγαπῶσι μᾶλλον τὰ αὑτῶν ἔργα, ὥσπερ οἱ γονεῖς καὶ οἱ ποιηταί.

d 7 οἵ τε γὰρ λεγόμενοι μῦθοι, etc. The myths intended are probably of two kinds : (1) ancient myths describing the punishment of famous enemies of the Gods, such as Tantalus ; (2) myths associated with the Orphic mysteries, and applicable to the whole of mankind. For a fuller discussion, see the Appendix to these notes.

e 3 καὶ αὐτὸς . . . ἠδίκηκεν. The punctuation of the words from ἤτοι to αὐτά as a parenthesis is due to Burnet. On the old view, with a full-stop after καθορᾷ αὐτά, the words ὑπὸ τῆς τοῦ γήρως ἀσθενειάς had to be somehow construed with καθορᾷ αὐτά ; but ' to regard the bodily weakness of old age as in itself the cause of clearer vision of the world beyond may be in harmony with the doctrine of the *Phaedo*, but Cephalus is not represented as a Platonist '. [Adam.]

αὐτά (l. 5) are, of course, τὰ ἐκεῖ.

ὥσπερ (l. 4) is appropriate, since we are not literally nearer to the next world in old age, any more than life is literally a journey.

δ'οὖν can be paraphrased ' whatever the truth may be.'

e 5 αὐτά, i.e. τὰ ἐκεῖ.

e 8 καὶ ἐκ τῶν ὕπνων . . . καὶ ζῇ ' both . . . and . . . .'

331 a 1 ἐλπίδος. Notice this use of ἐλπίς for the expectation of evil.

a 6 γλυκεῖα, etc. ' Sweet hope, making glad his heart, accompanies him as the nurse of his old age—hope, who ever directs the changing mind of mortal men.' The context is not known.

b 2 τὸ γὰρ . . . ἐξαπατῆσαι . . . μέγα μέρος εἰς τοῦτο. The grammatical case of τὸ ἐξαπατῆσαι is at first undetermined ; eventually the construction appears—it is an accusative in apposition to εἰς τοῦτο.

— μηδὲ ἄκοντά τινα ἐξαπατῆσαι. ἄκοντα is the subject, and τινα the object : ' never to have cheated another, even against one's will.' How can wealth protect a man from this ? Perhaps because the poor man can only pay the bare minimum of his debt whilst the rich man can sometimes afford to give others the benefit of the doubt. Moreover, a man might unconsciously incur a debt of sacrifice to the Gods, as many of the legends show. The rich man could afford to appease all the Gods on the ' hit or miss ' principle.

b 5 μέγα μέρος . . . συμβάλλεται, ' contributes in a high degree.'

b 7 οὐκ ἐλάχιστον : not an adverb, but an adjective agreeing with τοῦτο, ' it is not least for this purpose . . .' Plato introduces a second superlative, which is not really necessary, in χρησιμώτατον.

b 8 νοῦν ἔχοντι, ' reasonable ' or ' sensible '.
Νοῦς always has the sense of *intuitive* reason, as opposed to calculation or demonstration.

c 2 τὴν ἀλήθειαν, ' truthfulness '—a somewhat rare use of this word : cf. Arist. *Nic. Eth.*, ii, 1108 *a* 20.

c 3 ἁπλῶς οὕτως, ' in this absolute way.' ἁπλῶς denotes an *unqualified* statement.

c 7 σωφρονοῦντος, ' in his right mind,' opp. to μανείς. This is very near to the etymological sense of σωφρονεῖν. The common meaning, ' temperate,' is a later development.

c 10 ἐθέλων : ' willing ' or ' consenting '.

d 2 ὅρος and the more technical ὁρισμός both mean ' definition '. Like the Latin equivalent, they have originally a spatial sense.

d 4 μὲν οὖν : see 341 *a* 1 n.

d 5 Σιμωνίδη πείθεσθαι : The surviving fragments of Simonides are comparatively few, and they do not contain the statement about Justice which Polemarchus presently quotes.

d 8 Οὐκοῦν, ἔφη, ἐγώ, ὁ Πολέμαρχος. According to this punctuation, οὐκοῦν goes with ἐγώ and ἔφη with ὁ Πολέμαρχος : ' Well then,' said Polemarchus, ' am not I your heir ? ' Such an order of words, called *hyperbaton*, is seen at **d** 4 just above, and elsewhere. (Adam omits the comma at ἐγώ, ' Am not I, Polemarchus, your heir ? ' This makes the question sound rather affected. Others emend to ἔφην ἐγώ and attribute the question to Socrates.)

d 10 ᾔει πρὸς τὰ ἱερά : Cicero (*ad Atticum*, iv, 16, 3) makes an excellent remark on the retirement of Cephalus : ' Credo Platonem vix putasse satis consonum fore, si hominem id aetatis in tam longo sermone diutius retinuisset.'

331 d–336 a The argument with Polemarchus is examined in the Introduction.

e 5 δίκαιόν ἐστι, ' is just ' : to Polemarchus, who cannot distinguish between an instance of Justice and its definition, this means precisely the same as τὸ δίκαιόν ἐστι. The fallacy is more obvious in English—unless, indeed, we imitate Greek and speak of ' the Just '.

332 a 1 μὴ σωφρόνως. Cf. 331 c 7 n.

a 2 που, ' I presume '.

a 4 ὁπότε τις μὴ σωφρόνως ἀπαιτοῖ. Two explanations of the optative here are possible. It may be what is called an optative of indefinite frequency, serving to generalize the statement : ' whenever anyone asked.' Or it may be that the whole sentence is really in indirect speech in past sequence : ' (we admitted that) one ought by no means to restore . . .' The latter seems preferable.

a 9 φίλοις. ' Friend ' will normally serve as a translation of φίλος, and ' love ' of φιλεῖν ; but it should be noted that φιλία, unlike the English ' friendship ', includes the affection of near relatives.

a 12 μανθάνω, ' I understand.'

— ὅτι οὐ, etc. The punctuation here adopted is that of Burnet. ὅτι, meaning ' that ', occurs far in advance of λέγειν (b 3), on which it is logically and grammatically dependent.
Other editors place a colon at ἀποδιδούς (b 2) ; in this case the ὅτι must mean ' because '.

b 7 ὀφείλεται . . . ὅπερ καὶ προσήκει : Every step which Polemarchus makes is false. He here volunteers to alter the expression ' what is owed ' into ' what is becoming '. But these are not synonyms. Medical treatment, e.g., is ' becoming ' for an invalid. But, unless he has some right to expect it, it is not owed to him. The notion of τὸ προσῆκον is wider —and weaker—than that of τὸ ὀφειλόμενον.

c 4 'Αλλὰ τί οἴει ; ' A rhetorical question, which needs and receives no answer, like τί μήν ; and τί μὴν δοκεῖς ; (Theaet. 162 b).' (Adam.) Tr. ' of course '. If it had been a genuine question to Socrates, he could hardly have brushed it aside and gone on to a new point.

c 5 'Ω πρὸς Διός. Some editors take these words as part of the address to Simonides. They are, it is true, rather far ahead of ὦ Σιμωνίδη ; but this would be quite in Plato's manner. The word οὖν, however, would in this case be superfluous and awkward. If the phrase ὦ πρὸς Διός indicated strong surprise, it would certainly be more natural that Simonides should be the person addressed. But it means no more than the English 'good gracious ! '

c 6 ἀποδιδοῦσα. The sense of this word has altered slightly on account of the new equation between ' what is owed ' and ' what is becoming ' ; it is not now ' to restore ', but ' to assign what is due '.

c 9 φάρμακά τε καὶ σιτία καὶ ποτά. It would have been better to say ' Medicine assigns physical health to the body '. Polemarchus, however, characteristically takes the most superficial view. Notice his idea of a cure : he thinks of drugs and of diet, but does not mention surgery. Operations were sometimes performed (cf. καύσει ἢ τομῇ, ii, 406 *d*), but having no anaesthetics, and few means of stopping the flow of blood, doctors avoided them if possible. In Homer, wounds are generally treated by ἤπια φάρμακα.

Plato not only refers frequently to medical science for purposes of comparison, but shows interest in it for its own sake. Later, in Book III, he discusses it from the point of view of a legislator. In the *Timaeus* he states the function of various organs in the body, and the causes of disease, showing considerable knowledge of anatomy. There were in his day two great schools of medicine : that founded in the fifth century by Hippocrates of Cos, and that which had its centre at Croton (S. Italy). Plato was in close contact with the latter, and for the most part accepted its views. See the work of J. L. Heiberg on *Mathematics and Natural Science in Classical Antiquity*, (translated from the German by D. C. Macgregor.)

d 1   ἡ τοῖς ὄψοις τὰ ἡδύσματα. Elsewhere (*Gorgias*, 463 *a*) Plato refuses to classify ὀψοποιητική as an art at all—no doubt more in accordance with his real opinion.

Tr. ' the art which imparts the proper seasoning to dishes '. Ὄψα are dishes of either meat or vegetables, as contrasted with σιτία, bread or cakes. Ὄψον, however, has also a narrower sense than this, in which it refers to meat alone. (See Adam on *Rep.*, ii, 372 *c* 17.) The ἡδύσματα are condiments or sauces.

d 5   The repeated τε καί is a neat device for showing that benefit is owed to friends, and harm to enemies.

e 2   κυβερνήτης.   The κυβερνήτης was responsible not merely for the steering but also for the navigation of the ship.   If the owner was not on board, the steersman would probably take charge.   His art therefore demanded great skill and experience ; and the growth of naval warfare added a new complication, though this is not in Plato's mind here. Cf. the speech of Pericles in Thucyd. i, 142, 9 : τὸ δὲ ναυτικὸν τέχνης ἐστιν, ὥσπερ καὶ ἄλλο τι, καὶ οὐκ ἐνδέχεται ὅταν τύχῃ ἐκ παρέργου μελετᾶσθαι, ἀλλὰ μᾶλλον μηδὲν ἐκείνῳ πάρεργον ἄλλο γίγνεσθαι ... καί, ὅπερ κράτιστον, κυβερνήτας ἔχομεν πολίτας καὶ τὴν ἄλλην ὑπηρεσίαν πλείους καὶ ἀμείνους ἢ ἅπασα ἡ ἄλλη Ἑλλάς.

e 5   Προσπολεμεῖν applies to Justice in relation to enemies, συμμαχεῖν in relation to friends.

e 7   μὴ κάμνουσι . . . ἰατρὸς ἄχρηστος.   Here Pol. loses another chance.   Medicine, as the Greek doctors themselves insisted, is as useful in preserving health as in curing disease.

333 a 13   συμβόλαια, κοινωνήματα.   By the former term, Pol. meant any business contracts involving money.   Socrates, wishing, as Adam points out, to introduce once more the analogy of the arts, substitutes a still more general term, 'partnerships.' He also interprets κοινῇ in a way of his own. To Pol. it suggested the partnership *between buyer and seller*—and here it is plausible to say that Justice has a real use. Socrates' partnership is that of people owning money in common and making a joint purchase ; here Justice is still indispensable, but it is not so easy to say what it does. Hence arises a misunderstanding between the two speakers which persists throughout (see *c* 5, 7).

b 2 εἰς πεττῶν θέσιν. Suffice it to say that this was a game resembling chess or backgammon or draughts. θέσις apparently meant a move in the game. It was known to the suitors in the household of Odysseus :

οἱ μὲν ἔπειτα

πεσσοῖσι προπάροιθε θυράων θυμὸν ἔτερπον   (Od. I. 107)

b 9 εἰς κρουμάτων : sc. κοινωνίαν. The κροῦμα is the *striking* of a note ; the strings were struck, not scraped. Cf. πλῆκτρον, from πλήττω.

c 7 καὶ σῶν εἶναι, 'and (for it) to be safe.' The first verb applies to the depositor, the second to the deposit.

d 4 καὶ κοινῇ καὶ ἰδίᾳ, 'both by oneself, and in partnership with others '—i.e. whether the object belongs to one person or to several. This seems to be simply an addition thrown in in order to confuse Polemarchus. It has never been clear in this argument whether the κοινωνία is between the depositor and the trustee, or between persons who jointly own a thing, and deposit it with someone else.

e 1, 2 σπουδαῖον, χρήσιμον, 'a serious *thing*,' 'a useful *thing*.'

e 5 φυλάξασθαι. The stages in this argument are : (1) he who can strike a blow, can also defend himself against one *(φυλάξασθαι)*. (2) he who can defend himself against a disease, can secretly give it to someone else ; (3) he who can surprise the enemy or steal their plans, can also guard his own camp against surprise (φύλαξ, 334 *a* 1). (4) Therefore, in general, whatever a man guards well, that he can steal. (φύλαξ, *a* 5 ; φυλάττειν, *a* 7). This arrangement is extraordinarily ingenious. How does Socrates reach the conclusion ὅτου τις ἄρα δεινὸς φύλαξ, τούτου καὶ φὼρ δεινός? Only by passing gradually from φυλάξασθαι (to defend oneself against) to φυλάττειν (to guard, keep, as in the phrase ' to keep money safe '.) Between these two senses a kind of middle term is found : the φύλαξ of the camp *both* guards against ' surprise, and keeps the camp safe. The transition required by the argument then becomes possible.

e 7 'Αρ' οὖν . . . ἐμποιήσας ; The word λαθεῖν is a subtle addition, which prepares for the conclusion that the just man is a thief. No reason has been given why either the onset or the defence should be *stealthy.*

'Εμποιήσας is the conjecture of Schneider for the ἐμποιῆσαι of the

mss. It seems to be inevitably required. The ms. reading may, be
due to the misunderstanding of some early copyist, who punctuated
after λαθεῖν and took this verb together with φυλάξασθαι, ' to guard
against and evade.'

334 a 2 κλέψαι governs both βουλεύματα and πράξεις, and is
therefore used in a wider sense than usual. It was used for ' military
operations involving surprise or stealth ' (Adam). Tr. ' to steal the
plans of the enemy, and outwit them in their operations '.

b 2 Αὐτόλυκον: This is based on *Od.* xix, 395 :—μητρὸς ἑῆς πατέρ'
ἐσθλόν, ὃς ἀνθρώπους ἐκέκαστο κλεπτοσύνῃ θ' ὅρκῳ τε.
The statement that Homer ' loves ' Autolycus rests entirely on the
adjective ἐσθλόν. Ὅρκος here = the making of an oath with intent to
break it.

b 9 ἡ δικαιοσύνη : τοῦτο is the original subject of δοκεῖ, ' this
still seems to me to be true.' It is then displaced, and δικαιοσύνη
brought in as the subject.

d 13 ὅσοι διημαρτήκασι τῶν ἀνθρώπων, ' those who have completely
(δι-) misjudged their men.' Ἀμαρτάνειν is to miss the mark (opp. to
τυγχάνειν). It is followed by a genitive of the object missed or
misjudged.

e 1 αὐτοῖς ' for them,' i.e. in their eyes—an ethic dative. Some
commentators insist that, at this point in the argument, the contrast
between opinion and reality is no longer in place ; they therefore
take αὐτοῖς as possessive dative, ' for they have bad enemies.' But
this is unnatural, and it is not necessitated by the argument. When
Pol. agreed, in *d* 10, that it was just to harm the unjust, and assist
the just, he still meant *those whom one thinks* unjust and just. It is not
until 335 *a* that he introduces the refinement τὸν δοκοῦντά τε καὶ τὸν
ὄντα χρηστόν.

e 3 αὐτὸ τοὐναντίον ' the very reverse.'

e 10 The second τόν seems somewhat out of place in this expression.
The sense required is ' one who both seems and is '.

335 a 6 [ἢ] ὡς τὸ πρῶτον ἐλέγομεν : ' (to add to the definition
of Justice) as we first formulated it.' It is best here to bracket ἢ ; but
it may be well to explain what the construction would be if it were
retained. (1) ἢ may mean ' or, in other words ' ; ὡς τὸ πρῶτον ἐλέγομεν
is, as it must be on any view, a reminder of the old definition ; and
this phrase is then resumed in the single word τούτῳ, l. 8. (2) it may
mean " than ", following on the notion of enlargement or being-greater-
than which is implied in προσθεῖναι. Neither of these explanations is
attractive ; the former seems less unlikely.

b 6 δεῖ βλάπτειν. The emphasis here is on δεῖ. To Pol. enemies, and ' bad men ' generally, are by definition people whom one *should* harm.

βλάπτειν, like our ' to injure ', has a double sense : with a personal object, it means ' to do injustice to ', with an impersonal one, ' to spoil.' This makes possible the following refutation.

b 8 Ἄρα εἰς τὴν τῶν κυνῶν ἀρετήν, etc. εἰς = ' with reference to ', the ἀρετή being viewed as a limit by which progress is measured.

According to the explanation of ἀρετή given in a later passage (353 *b*), and implied everywhere in Plato, the ἀρετή of a thing is determined by its proper function, οἰκεῖον ἔργον. The eyes are designed for seeing ; and good sight, the ἀρετή of the eyes, enables them to see well. The same is true of every being, living or inanimate, natural or artificial. From this it is obvious that ἀρετή is applied more extensively than the English or Latin *virtue*, which tend to be confined to goodness of human character. But Plato correctly interprets and closely follows the ordinary Greek usage ; and Polemarchus would instinctively understand the word in the sense which is given to it in the later passage.

What, it may be asked, do the parties to the present argument understand by the ἀρετή of a dog or a horse ? Is it something fixed by nature, or something relative to a service which these animals perform for man ? It may be answered that these are not true alternatives : for though the animals are chosen by man for a particular work, the choice is not arbitrary, and takes account of their natural capabilities. Aristotle considers that the ἀρετή of a horse is displayed in ' running, carrying its rider, and facing the enemy ' (*N.E.* ii 6, 2). These are qualities demanded from the horse by men, but only because they see that the horse is naturally fitted to provide them. Even the Sophists would not have carried the antithesis between νόμος and φύσις to the point of maintaining that man normally perverts the course of nature—though it may be added that Rousseau, in modern times, was often inclined to think so : see the opening of his Émile : ' Tout est bien sortant des mains de l'Auteur des choses, tout dégénère entre les mains de l'homme. Il force une terre à nourrir les productions d'une autre, un arbre à porter les fruits d'un autre ; il ne veut rien tel que l'a fait la nature, pas même l'homme.'

c 1 Ἀνθρώπους . . . μὴ οὕτω φῶμεν, ' are we not to say the same of men ? ' Supply ' that ' before βλαπτομένους.

d 6 ξηρότητος, etc. 'Dry,' ξηρόν, and moist, ὑγρόν, were favourite notions of medical writers in their speculation about the conditions necessary to health. This may have suggested the choice of this instance.

e 2 τοῦτο . ..νοεῖ αὐτῷ, ' and he means by this,' lit. ' and this means for him.' αὐτῷ is an ethic dative ; cf. αὐτοῖς, 334 *e* 2.

e 5 οὐδαμοῦ γὰρ δίκαιον οὐδένα ἡμῖν ἐφάνη ὂν βλάπτειν: *Hurt* may be inflicted, in the form of punishment, but being designed to effect improvement, this hurt is not *harm*.   Later, Plato says that if the Gods are represented by poets as causing pain to men, it must be shown that they are punishing them for their own good.

e 9 *Βίαντα, Πιττακόν*: famous wise men who lived early in the sixth century B.C.

336 a 5 *Περιάνδρου*: he too was normally included among the company of Wise Men.   But he was also famous as a despotic ruler, who ruthlessly cut down his rivals (Herodotus, v, 92).   He was tyrant of Corinth in the seventh century.

— *Περδίκκου*: some Macedonian king, perhaps one who died about 413 B.C.   An Archelaus, son of Perdiccas, is mentioned in the *Gorgias* as an unscrupulous tyrant.

a 6 *Ἰσμηνίου*: a Theban well known to have received large bribes from the Persians (Xenophon, *Hellenica*, iii, 5, 1).   Plato mentions him also in the *Meno*, 90 a.   The misdeeds of Ismenias did not occur until after the death of Socrates, but Plato, in the warmth of his disapproval, defies chronology.   (This is denied, without sufficient grounds, by Wilamowitz, *Platon*, ii, p. 104.)

a 7 *οἰομένου*: To the philosopher, the power which such men *think* they have is imaginary : cf. *Gorgias*, 467 a.

b 1 *καὶ διαλεγομένων ἡμῶν μεταξύ*, ' actually during our conversation.'   He tried to ' seize the argument ', but was then (*ἔπειτα*) restrained by his neighbours.   The imperfect *ὥρμα* helps to show that he did not succeed.
Notice in this sentence several compounds of *διά* : *διακοῦσαι* ' to hear *to the end*, *διεπαυσάμεθα* ' we had *quite* finished ' etc.

b 6 *ἧκεν*, not ' he came at us ', from *ἥκω*—this idiom is purely English—but ' he threw himself upon us ', from *ἵημι*.

b 7 *πτοεῖσθαι* is to be excited, *διαπτοεῖσθαι* to be panic-stricken. Like the English ' flutter ', they are originally applied to birds.

c 1 *εὐηθίζεσθε* : there is no quality which Thras. so much despises as what he calls ' simplicity '—cf. 343 c 7, 348 c 12.

c 2 *ὑποκατακλινόμενοι*. *Κατακλίνεσθαι* is to recline, *ὑποκατακλίνεσθαι* to recline in a lower place from deference to someone else ; hence this metaphorical use.   The active *κατακλίνειν* means to offer a seat, as a mark of respect : cf. iv 425 b 2.   Others suggest with less plausibility that the metaphor here is borrowed from a ' ducking ' movement in wrestling.

c 4 *μηδὲ φιλοτιμοῦ ἐλέγχων*, ' do not try to make yourself popular by your criticism of others.'

c 7 *καὶ ὅπως*. We must understand *σκοπεῖ*, or some similar word :— hence the ensuing *μή*.   This idiom would only be used by an impolite person, or one talking to his inferiors.

d 7 ἄφωνος ἄν γενέσθαι. A man meeting a wolf was supposed to be struck dumb if it saw him first. Cf. Vergil, *Ecl.* ix, 53 ' vox quoque Moerim Iam fugit ipsa, lupi Moerim videre priores '.

e 4 τῶν λόγων, i.e. the arguments used, which Socrates and Polemarchus have been jointly examining.

e 5 ἄκοντες ἁμαρτάνομεν. Socrates maintained two paradoxical opinions, firstly that no one voluntarily errs, οὐδεὶς ἑκὼν ἁμαρτάνει, and secondly that it is better to err on purpose than against one's will, ὁ ἑκὼν ἁμαρτάνων αἱρετώτερος. The foundation of both views was the same : men ought to act under the guidance of reason and judgment ; and they do in fact always make the best use of such intelligence as they have. There is no such thing as a *desire* to do what one knows to be *bad* ; only the good can be desired ; but a man may misjudge the nature of the good, or may miscalculate the means of obtaining a good end. All error is intellectual. Now a man who makes such a mistake, but fails to see it, is less perfect than one who deliberately makes the mistake (this was the second paradox), and he acts *against his will*, since if he received knowledge he would immediately choose otherwise and his mistake concerns the means, not the end (this was the first paradox).

— μὴ γὰρ δὴ etc. This is an argument *a fortiori*, that is to say, a less impressive instance (εἰ μὲν χρυσίον ἐζητοῦμεν) is used to prove a stronger one (δικαιοσύνην δέ). The form is a favourite one with Plato : cf. *Phaedo* 68 a, *Laws* 931 c.

e 6 ἑκόντας εἶναι, ' willingly.' The εἶναι adds nothing to the sense, but is sometimes added to ἑκών by Greek idiom after a negative.

e 7 διαφθείρειν, ' ruin.'

e 11 οἷον γε σύ, i.e. believe me that we are striving hard to discover Justice. The οἷον here is quite unconnected with that in μὴ γὰρ δὴ οἷου, l. 4.

337 a 2 χαλεπαίνεσθαι, ' to be victims of your anger.' This passive form of a verb which, in the active, takes a dative of the person, is somewhat irregular. cf. Thucydides iv, 61, σύμπαντες ἐπιβουλευόμεθα.

a 3 ἀνεκάγχασε, ' broke into a harsh laugh ' : an onomatopoeic word, related to the Latin *cachinnor*. ἀνά, in such compounds, suggests a sudden beginning.

— σαρδάνιον. From this word, sometimes spelt σαρδόνιον comes the English ' sardonic '. Most probably it is related to σαίρειν and σεσηρέναι—to grin, showing the teeth at the same time ; hence σαρδόνιον might denote a laugh accompanied by a threat. Later Greek writers derive the word from Σαρδώ, Sardinia. There, they say, is found a bitter herb, the eating of which is followed by a convulsive laughter that may end in death (cf. *Sardoniis amarior herbis*, Vergil Ecl. 7, 41). ' Sarcasm ' is said to be derived from the verb σαρκάζω, to rend flesh with one's teeth.

a 5 εἰρωνεία. The Greek word means affectation of ignorance or inferiority ; cf. Theophrastus' definition, προσποίησις ἐπὶ χεῖρον πράξεών τε καὶ λόγων.

a 8 εἰ τίς τί σε ἐρωτᾷ. Why the sudden return to the indicative ? Perhaps the reason is that the εἰ is not genuinely conditional, but temporal, and temporal clauses are liable to such changes, which make for liveliness.

b 8 εἰ . . . τυγχάνει ὄν, 'if it really is one of these things.' τυγχάνειν, 'hit the mark,' is often so used of an apt statement or description. ῎Ον is emphatic.

b 9 ἕτερον . . . τοῦ ἀληθοῦς, not 'another part of the truth '—which would not make sense—but ' something other *than* the truth '.

c 2 ὡς δή is used with ironical intention ; its Latin equivalent would be *quasi vero*. [Denniston, *Greek Particles*, p. 229.]

c 7 ἄλλο τι οὖν, 'surely,' an idiomatic phrase used to introduce a question which expects the answer ' yes '.

d 2 τί ἀξιοῖς παθεῖν ; The key to this passage is a procedure in Athenian law called τίμησις and ἀντιτίμησις. In certain lawsuits, after a man had been found guilty, he would be required to answer the question, τί ἀξιοῖς παθεῖν ἢ ἀποτεῖσαι ; The penalty was not fixed, or was only fixed within certain limits, by the law, and the defendant would have a chance of pleading for a moderate penalty and escaping quite lightly.   This was the ἀντιτίμησις, ' counter-estimate,' (the accuser's estimate having been the τίμησις.)

Thrasymachus asks Socrates, ' what do you deserve to suffer ? ' Socrates, making a play on words (παθεῖν, μαθεῖν), says ' I deserve to be cured of my ignorance by someone who knows the truth '. Thrasymachus replies ' you are jesting ; in addition to learning, you must pay some money '.

The Sophists all took fees for their teaching, and Protagoras was said to have left it to the pupil to judge what the teaching received was worth. But Plato's satire is too malicious to be effective. It seems incredible that even a Sophist would ask for money in the middle of a conversation.

d 9 ἐπειδάν μοι γένηται : Socrates was a man of moderate means—he served in the army as a hoplite—but he was not rich enough to pay the enormous fees of the Sophists.

d 12 εἰσοίσομεν. ' will contribute,' whence the noun εἰσφορά (343 **d** 7).

e 3 λαμβάνῃ λόγον, ' may demand an explanation.' λαμβάνειν suggests a more active inquiry than the usual δέχεσθαι.

e 6 εἴη : With Burnet, I have kept the text given in the mss. εἰ is omitted before ἀπειρημένον, probably for two reasons : (1) it has occurred in the clause εἰ τι καὶ οἴεται, and its reappearance, though in fact required, would complicate the sentence, (2) μὴ εἰδὼς (l. 5) has the force of a condition, 'if he did not know, and did not profess to know.' It would be possible to omit εἴη. In that case ἀπειρημένον would be an accusative absolute, 'when it had been forbidden.'

338 c 1 ἄκουε δή, etc. On Thrasymachus' view of Justice, see the Introduction.

c 7 Πουλυδάμας : a famous athlete, born in Thessaly, and a winner at the Olympic games of 408 B.C. The παγκράτιον was a contest including combined wrestling and boxing : Aristotle, *Rhet.* I, 5, 14 : ὁ δὲ θλίβειν (δυνάμενος) καὶ κατέχειν παλαιστικός, ὁ δὲ ὦσαι ᾗ πληγῇ πυκτικός, ὁ δὲ ἀμφοτέροις τούτοις παγκρατιαστικός.

d 3 ὑπολαμβάνεις, 'you understand (one's meaning)'; Latin *suscipis*.

d 6 Plato himself was never satisfied with this simple classification of forms of government. He believes that there are not three forms but six—i.e. three sound forms, Kingship, Aristocracy, and Moderate Democracy, and three perversions, Tyranny, Oligarchy and Extreme Democracy (*Statesman*, 302-3). To Thrasymachus any government that is strong enough to survive must be sound.

e 7 τοῦτ' οὖν ἐστιν, ὦ βέλτιστε . . . συμφέρον : tr. 'this is what I mean, my good friend, by the statement that there is one standard of Justice in all cities.' For a similar use of λέγω cf. 332 d 7 : τὸ τοὺς φίλους ἄρα εὖ ποιεῖν καὶ τοὺς ἐχθροὺς κακῶς δικαιοσύνην λέγει. Adam places a comma at λέγω, thus reducing this word to its barest sense, 'this is the statement I make'; but this seems to be refuted by the ὃ λέγεις in the reply of Socrates a few lines below.

339 a 3 πανταχοῦ εἶναι τὸ αὐτὸ δίκαιον : a surprising thing for a Sophist to say. But Thras. does not mean that there are immutable laws of Justice—if he did, that would be the view that Justice exists φύσει ; he means that Justice is made what it is at each particular time and place by the will of the stronger ; and this is the view that it exists νόμῳ, φύσει δὲ μή.

b 8 οὐ καὶ πείθεσθαι μέντοι : οὐ suggests that the anticipated answer to the question is 'yes'; μέντοι, that this is a new point likely to have some qualifying effect (Tucker). Tr. 'Still, do you not say . . .'
Thras. does not at present say that it is *always* just for the weaker set to obey ; it need only be so when the law laid down by the rulers is really to their interest. But he soon admits the wider proposition that it is just for them to obey any command whatever (c 10, d 6).

e 3 ὅταν . . . προσέταξαν. The sense is clear, but the construction requires some scrutiny. (1) The phrase ὅταν . . . προσέταξαι depends not on ὡμολογῆσθαι, but on ποιεῖν. (2) Plato writes : whenever you say that it is just : but he *means* 'and when it is, as you say, just '.

e 6 συμβαίνειν αὐτὸ οὑτωσί, 'that the following situation should result.' αὐτό is vague ; it means the argument, or the case described by the argument ; and οὑτωσί is amplified in δίκαιον ... λέγεις. (Or we might omit the comma at οὑτωσί, with Madvig : αὐτό would then qualify τοὐναντίον, 'the very reverse,' and οὑτωσί would mean ' by such reasoning '.)

340 a 8, 10 Good instances of the elliptic use of γάρ in conversation. The speaker assumes an unexpressed ' yes ' or ' no '.

b 8 ὃ ἡγοῖτο. The optative is due to the imperfect ἔλεγεν. It might stand for either ὃ ἡγεῖται or ὃ ἂν ἡγῆται in direct speech. Probably Cleitophon's loophole is rejected because Thrasymachus is, at present, trying to show that his view of Justice is natural, and quite independent of opinion.

c 3 ὃ ἐβούλου λέγειν τὸ δίκαιον, 'how you meant to define Justice.'

c 7 κρείττω με οἴει καλεῖν, etc. Notice that at this point Thras. accepts the comparison between ruling, i.e. Justice, and an art like medicine. It is also noticeable that he quickly veers round from his realism to the conception of an ideal infallibility.

d 1 συκοφάντης, a malicious accuser or ' informer '. On its derivation, see Liddell and Scott. Thras. treats his whole conversation with Socrates as a public display, so that any criticism of his argument amounts to an accusation brought by an informer.

d 2 αὐτίκα, ' for instance,' lit. immediately. The speaker professes to be quoting the first instance which occurs to him.

d 4 λογιστικόν, 'accountant' or 'calculator'. Λογιστική is opposed to the theoretical science of ἀριθμητική, which Plato would prefer to teach in an entirely non-practical spirit.

d 6 λέγομεν τῷ ῥήματι οὕτως, ' we use this form of words.'

d 7 The γραμματιστής was a teacher of writing and spelling ; he is not quite the same as the γραμματικός, i.e. the person who understands the rules of phonetics and the derivation of words.

— τὸ δ', ' whereas in fact . . .', a favourite Platonic idiom. Tucker traces its origin to the use of τὸ μέν and τὸ δέ to mark an antithesis, which we find in Herodotus. Τό refers to the whole statement, not to any noun which it contains.

e 2 ἐπειδὴ καί σύ ἀκριβολογῇ—an unfair remark, as it was Thras. who insisted that Socrates should be accurate.

e 3 ἐπιλειπούσης γὰρ ἐπιστήμης and ἐν ᾧ οὐκ ἔστι δημιουργός convey the same notion. For this reason it is desirable to read ἐπιλειπούσης, and not the aorist ἐπιλιπούσης with two of the mss.

e 6 εἴποι, 'would *say* ': cf. λέγομεν τῷ ῥήματι οὗτως, *d* 5.

e 8 ἀποκρίνεσθαι corresponds to an imperfect indicative : ' suppose this to be the answer which I *was trying to give*.'

e 9 τυγχάνει, see 337 *b* 7 n.

341 a 9 μὲν οὖν : cf. 331 *d* 4 n.

b 1 μὴ λαθών is conditional, ' if you don't take me by surprise.' Notice the omission of ἄν, which should normally accompany δύναιο, but is here understood from the previous clause.

b 4 διορίσαι : see note on ὅρος, 331 *d* 2.

b 6 ὡς ἔπος εἰπεῖν, ' to describe the thing in one word,' with the loss of accuracy which that sometimes entails : therefore ' in general ', ' approximately ', ' the ruler so called '.

— ἢ . . . νυνδὴ ἔλεγες ' or the ruler in what you recently called the accurate sense '.

b 11 οὐδέν σου παρίεμαι, ' I ask no mercy from you.' Παριέναι (ἁμάρτημα or βλάβην) is to forgive : παρίεσθαι, to ask for forgiveness. σου is dependent on παρά. There is a slight irregularity, as παρά is already doing its duty as a component in παριέναι.

— οὐ μὴ οἷός τ' ᾖς, ' you are not likely to be able (to injure my argument).'

e 1 ξυρεῖν λέοντα : a proverbial expression, no doubt the source of the English ' to beard a lion '.

c 3 οὐδὲν ὢν καὶ ταῦτα. Two translations are possible. (1) ' And that, too, though you are a worthless fellow.' οὐδὲν εἶναι is to be a mere cypher, a hopeless failure ; and καὶ ταῦτα makes a surprising fact seem more surprising than ever. (2) ' Though in that respect also you were a worthless fellow,' *viz.* in your first attempt to upset my definition. But the former is unlikely ; the position of καὶ ταῦτα would be unnatural.

d 6, 9 ἑκάστῳ τούτων . . . ἑκάστῳ : these datives are masculine, and refer to the persons who practise the arts—the steersman, doctor and so forth. There has been no mention yet of objects whose welfare the arts secure.

d 11 'Αρ' οὖν . . . τελέαν εἶναι : At this point we must begin to distinguish the art itself from the person who practises it. As will be seen later (346 *a* foll.) Socrates holds that such expressions as ' the doctor makes profits ' or ' the steersman earns wages ' are misleading.

As a doctor, a man is concerned solely with curing ; as a steersman, with the safety of the ship. It is not in his capacity as a representative of his craft that he earns money, for in that case the same art or craft would be enabling him to do two things at once.

This is what S. has in mind in his present question, ' Has each of the arts some further *advantage*, beyond its own greatest possible perfection ? ' This is highly abstract—but it is Thrasymachus whom we have to thank for the idea of a σκέψις τῷ ἀκριβεῖ λόγῳ.

e 5 νῦν ηὑρημένη, 'has now '—in our advanced stage of civilization —' been found '.

e 6 πονηρόν should be translated ' defective ', ' faulty '. So at 342 *a* 1.

e 7 τοιούτῳ, i.e. πονηρῷ. ' The body is liable to defect, and of this defect it requires to be cured,' *lit.* it is not enough for it to be of such a kind. Some editors consider that τοιούτῳ stands for σώματι : ' The body is defective, and merely being a body does not give it all that it requires,' i.e. it requires to be not merely a body, but a healthy body.

— ἐπὶ τούτῳ, ' for this purpose.'

342 a 1 foll. αὐτὴ ἡ ἰατρική, etc. We have just seen that if the body is to perform its function well, there must be an art which provides it with its proper ἀρετή, namely health. The same is true of any separate organ of the body, the eye, for instance (ὥσπερ . . . ἐκποριούσης). What of the art itself ? Has that also an ἀρετή which must be provided for it from outside ? If so, either (i) we must postulate a second art, whose function it is to give ἀρετή to the first, and a third whose function it is to give ἀρετή to the second, and so on *ad infinitum*, or (ii) we must suppose that the first art provides its own ἀρετή in addition to the ἀρετή of the body which it is its primary business to consider. But how can one art do two things ? These difficulties may be avoided if we say that the ἀρετή of an art is spontaneously secured when it attends most efficiently to its work. Medical science becomes *good* medical science when a body is cured.

a 2 ἀρετῆς : cf. the argument beginning at 352 *d*.

b 5 αὐτὴ δὲ ἀβλαβὴς καὶ ἀκέραιός ἐστιν ὀρθὴ οὖσα, ἕωσπερ ἂν ᾖ ἑκάστη [ἀκριβὴς] ὅλη ἥπερ ἐστίν ; *lit.* ' but each, by being correct (ὀρθή) is in itself faultless and unimpaired, so long as, taken in the accurate sense, it is entirely what it is.'

The main clause, down to οὖσα, needs no special explanation. The ἕωσπερ clause is meant to expand ὀρθὴ οὖσα, on lines which we already know. Ὅλη follows after ᾖ, to which it is the predicate, ' so long as it is wholly, i.e. nothing but, the art it is.' (E.g. the doctor's art, unadulterated by his desire to make money, which does not belong to him *as a doctor*.) This is what ' accurate ', ἀκριβής, means throughout this passage : cf. 342 *d* 7, 346 *b* 3. The word ἀκριβής, however, is doubly awkward here : (1) grammatically it must stand for ἀκριβὴς οὖσα, ' being taken in the accurate sense ' ; (2) the very next line repeats the injunction to ἀκρίβεια. I have preferred, therefore, to bracket this word as a gloss. (Dr. A. W. Pickard-Cambridge proposes ἀκριβῶς ὅλη etc., ' is entirely itself in the strict sense.')

c 8 ἄρχουσι . . . καὶ κρατοῦσι : Here the vagueness of τὸ κρεῖττον comes to the assistance of Socrates. The order of the argument is : (1) The arts aim at the welfare of their objects. (2) The arts are ' in command or control of ' those objects, (κρατεῖν, κρείττων). (3) Therefore, in so far as he has ἐπιστήμη, a ruler aims at the welfare of those he commands.

d 7 ἀκριβής : see 342 *b* 5 n.

e 9 ᾧ ἂν αὐτὸς δημιουργῇ is an expansion of τῷ ἀρχομένῳ ' the subject of his craft.'

343 a 2 ὁ τοῦ δικαίου λόγος, ' the definition of Justice,' i.e. that propounded by Thrasymachus.

a 8 αὐτῇ : the dative implies that Socrates' ignorance is to her discredit : ' she cannot even teach you to distinguish the sheep from the shepherd.' Notice the difference between οὐδέ, not even, and οὔτε, neither.

a 10 ὅτι δὴ τί μάλιστα, ' why exactly do you ask ? '

b 4 δεσποτῶν cannot mean ' owners ' (of the sheep)—it always refers to rule exercised over men by a man. It must refer, then, to masters who employ shepherds to watch their sheep. The shepherd looks after the flock for the profit of his master—and, indirectly, his own (τὸ τῶν δεσποτῶν ἀγαθὸν καὶ τὸ ἑαυτῶν). (Possibly καί is used in the sense of ἤ—' or, if they are his sheep, his own good '.)

b 5 ἄρχοντας, οἱ ὡς ἀληθῶς ἄρχουσιν : Thrasymachus, always the practised rhetorician, reiterates his idea of ' accuracy ' at the very point where he is going to abandon it. Two observations may be made on his long speech. (1) Once more he becomes the hard man of the world, who insists on taking people as they are with all their imperfections. His course has been very unsteady, alternating between fact and pedantic theory. Socrates justly charges him with inconsistency (345 c) : τὸν ὡς ἀληθῶς ἰατρὸν τὸ πρῶτον ὁριζόμενος τὸν ὡς ἀληθῶς ποιμένα οὐκέτι ᾤου δεῖν ὕστερον ἀκριβῶς φυλάξαι. Each disputant has his own reason for insisting on ' accurate definition ' : Thras., because the ruler in the strict sense makes no mistakes, Socrates because the ruler in the strict sense earns no profits. (2) During the speech Thras. passes on to a completely new idea—that all men really covet and admire Injustice, and are only deterred from it by the reproach and punishment which it brings. Hitherto Thras. has not said this :

he has only said that it is natural for the stronger to dictate to the weaker. This change also is emphasized by Socrates in his reply (347 *e*).

What exactly is the new position? It is that men do not at heart dislike and despise Injustice, as may be seen from the admiration which they express wherever it is practised on a large scale in the case of a successful tyrant. The reason for this is that most people are mediocre in their talents and strength, so that if there were universal freedom to commit Injustice they would lose more than they would gain. Unless one is a very strong man, one is better off under the reign of law : law is indeed a curb inflicted on the few strong men by the average multitude. This resembles the view of the transition from the state of nature to that of civil society which was expressed by certain philosophers of the seventeenth and eighteenth century, notably Thomas Hobbes. Plato does not mean us to feel that it is adequately refuted, or even adequately stated, in this introductory book. The view that there is selfishness involved in all human motives is capable of a much more plausible statement than Thras. here gives it.

b 7 διατεθείη 'might be disposed'. **Cf.** the noun διάθεσις, ' disposition '.

c 1 ὠφελήσονται : a middle form with a passive sense : for a list of similar cases, see Tucker's edition.

— οὔτω πόρρω εἶ περὶ τοῦ δικαίου, etc.
As πόρρω may mean either ' far advanced in ' or ' far away from ', two renderings are possible : (i) ' So profoundly versed are you in justice and injustice, that you are unaware . . .' (ii)—without the irony—' You are so far from knowing the true state of affairs about justice . . .' On the latter view we should have to supply τοῦ εἰδέναι after πόρρω εἶ.

c 2 τοῦ δικαίου καὶ δικαιοσύνης. The first is Justice as a quality of actions ; the second as a quality of persons. This discussion aims at a definition of Justice in the first sense, but only in order to see what it is in the second sense.

c 4 τῷ ὄντι, ' in reality,' is generally taken with ἀλλότριον ἀγαθόν ; but I prefer to punctuate after ἀγαθόν and make τῷ ὄντι the opening of the next phrase. For its occurrence in this position cf. *Phaedrus* 238 *c*.

c 6 καὶ ἄρχει. The subject is ὁ ἄδικος, which has to be supplied from ἀδικία. This is proved by ἐκείνου in the next line.

c 7 εὐηθικῶν : cf. 336 *c* 1, 348 *c* 12. The word εὐηθής, meaning by derivation ' of good character ', came to be employed in a sarcastic sense, ' simple,' ' foolish.'

d 3 ἐν τοῖς πρὸς ἀλλήλους συμβολαίοις, ' in dealings between man and man,' contrasted with ἐν τοῖς πρὸς τὴν πόλιν (*d* 6).

d 8 εἰσφοραί were not regular taxes, but contributions for special purposes imposed upon citizens and μέτοικοι in proportion to their property. The ἄδικος would show his skill by evading a just assessment.

d 9 λήψεις might refer to exceptional distributions of land or money, and, as the next sentence shows, it also includes the rewards of an official position.

e 7 τῷ δὲ ἀδίκῳ . . . ὑπάρχει, 'the unjust man can count on'. ὑπάρχει expresses the conditions, advantageous or the reverse, with which one is confronted in any undertaking.

344 a 3 τὸ δίκαιον, sc. εἶναι. δίκαιον is masculine.

a 6 οὐκ ἂν ἐθέλοντας We might expect the negative to be μή ; but οὐκ ἐθέλειν is treated as a single word.

a 7 ἢ οὐ . . . ἀλλὰ συλλήβδην. I retain the traditional text here, but feel that the sense would be much improved by transferring the words καὶ βίᾳ to the end of the sentence. The main contrast is between crime in a small way and the wholesale injustice of the tyrant ; and there is, I believe, a minor contrast between secret crime (λάθρᾳ) and violence (βίᾳ). What the sentence at present expresses is that injustice of either degree can be done either by stealth or by force, and no doubt this is true. But the tyrant has no need to be stealthy in his 'comprehensive' injustice (συλλήβδην), and the wrongdoer on a small scale is seldom in a position to use violence.

The place of the words καὶ ἱερὰ καὶ ὅσια καὶ ἴδια καὶ δημόσια is also suspicious. They also, as the sentence stands, give a catalogue of injustices of either degree. Thrasymachus' point is, in any case, that the small-scale wrong-doer can only commit these injustices one by one, and is abused and punished, whereas the tyrant can commit them all together, and is admired.

As regards the contrast between ἱερὰ and ὅσια, Tucker quotes Demosthenes *Timocr.*, 702 τῶν ἱερῶν μὲν τοὺς θεούς, τῶν ὁσίων δὲ τὴν πολίν ἀποστερεῖ; his comment is that things which can only be used for sacred and religious purposes are ἱερά ; things which it is 'lawful' or 'consistent with piety' to use for profane purposes are ὅσια.

b 5 τῶν τοιούτων κακουργημάτων is probably a genitive of respect, following on καλοῦνται and indicating why they are called by such names. It may, however, depend upon μέρη or upon ἀδικοῦντες.

b 7 ἀνδραποδισάμενος, 'enslaving.' The ἀνδραποδιστής mentioned in *b* 3 is one who kidnaps people to be sold into slavery. In general δοῦλοι meant those who were born as slaves, ἀνδράποδα those who became slaves after capture in war. Here ἀνδραποδισάμενος δουλώσηται may be translated ' he enslaves, and makes them his servants'. The first word, as Tucker points out, conveys the idea of seizing someone, the second that of turning him into a slave.

b 8 *κέκληνται.* Notice that the *τις* mentioned in the *ἐπειδάν* clause has here become plural. A moment later the singular is restored (*αὐτόν*).

c 7 *καὶ ὅπερ . . . συμφέρον.* 'And as I said at the beginning. Justice really is the advantage of the stronger, and Injustice is something profitable to oneself and advantageous.' These are intended to be definitions, but the latter is phrased as if it were simply a description, *τό* being omitted before *ἑαυτῷ.* The fact is that Thras. cannot offer a definition of Injustice because he has no consistent notion of it. Logically it ought to mean for him either *τὸ τοῦ ἥττονος συμφέρον* or *τὸ τοῦ κρείττονος ἀσύμφορον.* He has, however, introduced a fresh complication by calling the strong man *unjust*; he seems to want to use 'justice' in the sense of his definition, but to continue to use 'injustice' in the ordinary sense.

d 4 *ὑπομεῖναί τε καὶ παρασχεῖν λόγον.* The first of these verbs means 'remain, stand his ground'; it is intransitive, and does not govern *λόγον.* In an appropriate context, *ὑπομένειν* may, of course, be transitive ('submit to'). As to *παρασχεῖν,* it probably means the same as the more usual *διδόναι,* 'to offer an explanation of his words.'

e 1 The question to Cephalus, 'What do you consider to be the chief benefit of wealth?' led to a discussion, apparently theoretical, about the meaning of Justice. Thrasymachus has brought out an urgently practical question by his insistence that Justice is in itself less desirable than Injustice. Burnet prefers the reading *ὅλου* to *ἀλλ᾽ οὐ,* doubtless because it renders *ἐπιχειρεῖν* impersonal, whereas with *ὅλου* the subject 'you' or 'we' must be supplied.

e 2 *ᾗ, sc. ὁδῷ,* 'how.'

e 6 *Ἔοικας,* etc. Thras. asks 'Do I deny that this is so?' Socrates replies 'You appear to do so, or else to take no interest in us'.

345 a 1 *οὔτοι κακῶς σοι κείσεται,* 'will be no bad investment for you.' *Κεῖσθαι* is used of money invested to secure interest (*τοκός*).

a 7 *λανθάνειν, διαμάχεσθαι* : to succeed by stealth or by force : the antithesis is the old one between *λάθρᾳ* and *βίᾳ,* 344 *a.*

a 5-7 *ἀλλ᾽ . . . κερδαλεώτερον.*—a rather loosely constructed sentence. The subject of *ἔστω* is evidently the person whom Thrasymachus mentioned in his long speech, *viz.* the *τις* (344 *b* 5) who achieves 'complete injustice'. He is also the subject of *πείθει,* 'his example does not persuade me,' whereas the subject of *ἐστι* in l. 7 is, of course, *ἀδικία.* There is no need for the conjecture *πείθεις,* as *πείθει* is quite natural.

b 7 *ἐνθῶ,* from *ἐντίθημι,* 'am I to bring the argument and put it into your mind?'

c 2 ὁριζόμενος, 'though you *wished to* define'—representing an imperf. indic. The case is similar to that of ἀποκρίνεσθαι at 340 ε 7.

c 6 ἑστιάσεσθαι, probably in a passive sense, 'to enjoy a feast' (cf. 343 c 1 n.) Some translators (Lindsay, Davies and Vaughan) prefer the active 'to give a banquet'.

d 1-3 τῇ δὲ ποιμενικῇ, etc. A repetition of the point that an art is perfect when it attends perfectly to the welfare of its object (342 b).

d 5 οὕτω δὲ ᾤμην ἔγωγε νυνδή, 'for these reasons I concluded just now.'

e 1 καὶ θεραπευομένῳ. By this addition, as Tucker points out, Socrates begs the question. Θεραπεύειν would normally imply the care of persons or things in their own interest.

e 8 ὡς ἐσομένην. An accusative absolute construction — see Goodwin, *Greek Moods and Tenses*, § 110. Such a construction must be introduced by ὡς, unless certain impersonal verbs, ἐξόν, δέον, etc., are used.

346 a 4 παρὰ δόξαν, 'contrary to your real opinion.' Evidently Thras. was renowned for this—cf. 350 e. The phrase could also mean 'contrary to the general opinion', 'sensational'—hence the English 'paradox'.

b 1 μισθωτική, 'the art of profit.' As the argument shows, this includes both the earning of μισθός in the narrower sense (wages, hire), and the making of profit in general (κέρδος).

b 4 ὑπέθου, 'proposed at the beginning,' from ὑποτίθεσθαι. A ὑπόθεσις is an assumption agreed upon at the start and used as a basis for argument.

— ἐάν τις κυβερνῶν ὑγιὴς γίγνηται etc. By going to sea as a steersman, a man may restore himself to health, but it will not be in virtue of the art of steering that he becomes healthy (Logicians—following Aristotle—would describe this as a case of causation *per accidens*.) Again, a man may obtain health by exercising a profitable profession (l. 8 ἐὰν ὑγιαίνῃ τις μισθαρνῶν), or may obtain profit whilst restoring others to health (l. 10 ἐὰν ἰώμενός τις μισθαρνῇ), but medicine and profit-making are not to be confused.

To some extent this is a valid argument. But (1) what of the numerous occupations which are intrinsically pleasant? Surely this pleasure is a 'reward', a motive for choosing the occupation; yet it is not external to the occupation and so is not covered by Socrates' present argument. A doctor's motive in healing might be the pleasure which he derived from his own skill and success. (2) Again, his motive might be the love of money, and it might be agreed that this had no bearing on his capacity as a doctor, but still the idea of an art of profit is far-fetched. In practice the professional worker obeys mixed motives. A doctor whose thoughts were entirely engrossed by the profits he was going to make could scarcely be said to possess the art of medicine ; and one who completely dismissed from his mind the thought of money, but sent in his bill afterwards, could scarcely be said to have exercised an *art* of profit-making. However we look at it, it is difficult to represent the acquisition of profits by whole-hearted attention to one's business as an *art*.

b 5 συμφέρον. The Vienna ms. 55 (' F ') which is valuable to us as the sole representative of an independent tradition, reads συμφέρειν. συμφέρον is the reading of all other mss., including A (Parisinus 1807, one of the two most important mss. of Plato which exist). I agree with Burnet in preferring the more difficult συμφέρον, and taking it as accus. absolute (cf. 345 *e* 8 n.). The article τὸ belongs to πλεῖν.

c 5 ῞Ηντινα, etc. ' If there is some benefit enjoyed by all craftsmen in common, clearly they must employ some additional faculty, common to all, and derive the benefit from that.' ᾽Εκείνου is the κοινόν τι just mentioned. Notice προσχρῆσθαι, ' to use in addition.'

c 9 Notice δέ γε introducing the second of two premisses to an argument (see Denniston, *The Greek Particles*, p. 154). The force of γε is ' as you remember ', but it is best to leave it untranslated.

e 4 τέχνη οὐδ'ἀρχή.   Cf. 342 *c* 8 n.   The assumption made throughout this argument is not exactly that ruling is one of the arts, but that all the arts are varieties of rule, since each supervises some object and provides for its health or welfare.

e 9 μηδένα : μή tends to be used in sentences expressing a doubt or denial, or even, as here, a tentative assertion.

347 a 8 ὡς = ὅπως, ' in what sense.'

b 7 πραττόμενοι, ' exacting.'

b 9 οὐ γάρ εἰσι φιλότιμοι, ' they are not covetous of honour.' The best men would not be insensitive to honour, but it would not be their chief inducement to action.

d 2 πόλις ἀνδρῶν ἀγαθῶν εἰ γένοιτο : The trait mentioned here is reproduced in the State which Plato designs in Books II–VII. The most desirable life is that of philosophy, which demands leisure from practical life and the duties of administration ; but when it is his turn to fulfil these duties, the citizen will not disobey the command of the law (520 *a*). The present passage is not, of course, a full anticipation of the later one. We still have no positive conception of Justice. Here, Plato says that the just man consents to rule because he will otherwise be ruled by his inferiors ; there, that he cannot disobey the command of the State which has made him what he is.

The intervention of Glaucon in the discussion, precisely where there is this allusion to the sequel, is very significant. It must suggest to every observant reader that Plato planned Book I as an introduction to the remainder of the *Republic*.

e 3 ὁ νῦν λέγει Θρασύμαχος. See note on 343 *b* 5.

348 a 7 ἀντικατατείναντες. Cf. 329 *e* 9, also Book II 358 *d* : διὸ κατατείνας ἐρῶ τὸν ἄδικον βίον ἐπαινῶν. Originally a transitive verb, κατατείνειν comes to have an intransitive sense, 'strain,' Ἀντι means in competition with Thrasymachus.

b 3 ἀνομολογούμενοι, 'reaching an agreement with each other.'

c 12 γενναίαν εὐήθειαν. γενναῖος etymologically means 'well-born.' It is generally metaphorical and ironical in Plato : cf. μάζας γενναίας 372 *b*, 'noble cakes,' γενναία τυραννίς 544 *c*, 'splendid tyranny.' Here ' sublime simplicity ' : on εὐήθεια see 343 *c* 7 n.

Notice how perplexing to Thras. is the question whether Justice should be classified as κακία. He cannot give a direct answer because of a fundamental ambiguity in his use of the terms ' just ' and ' unjust '. His first definition said that it was just for the subjects to obey the commands given to them by their rulers for selfish reasons, but omitted to say whether the rulers who issue these commands were just. It was certainly implied that they were. But when shaken in his first argument, Thras. went on to describe the strong man or tyrant as unjust, and to flout justice altogether (see 344 *c* 7 n.).

His position ought to be this : to issue commands, and insist on obedience to them, is δικαιοσύνη so long as one is really stronger, and therefore ἀρετή : to disobey commands, on any other ground than that one is stronger than the person who gave them, is ἀδικία and therefore κακία.

d 1 κακοήθειαν, 'badness of character '—a word not in current use, but coined to match εὐήθεια.

d 6 ἔθνη : nations who live scattered about the country, as opposed to those who live in cities (πόλεις).

d 7 βαλλάντια. Purses worn hanging from a girdle, and so liable to be cut away by thieves : Latin *marsupium*.

e 2 ἐθαύμασα. ' I am surprised '—a gnomic aorist : cf. ἔμαθον, 339 *a* 5

e 5 στερεώτερον, 'a more stubborn position.' In its literal sense, στερεόν is ' hard ' or ' solid ' : in mathematics στερεά are solids, opp. to ἐπίπεδα, planes : cf. 528 *a* 9.

e 8 ὡμολογεῖς : this imperfect indicates a time less remote than the pluperfect ἐτίθεσο.

349 a 1 προσετίθεμεν, ' have been used to ascribe.'

b 1 ἀλλὰ τόδε, etc. In this passage Socrates catches his opponent out by making him admit various separate points, and suddenly putting these together.

The first stage of the argument extends down to *d* 11. A just man would not attempt to 'surpass' another just man, or a just action ; but, if he were free to do so, he would surpass an unjust man. The unjust man on his side would try to surpass everyone, both those who resemble him in character and those who do not. ('Surpass' is not a full equivalent to πλεονεκτεῖν. It is too neutral a word, the Greek having an implication of deceit and unfairness. Socrates' refutation depends on this fact : at one point πλεονεκτεῖν denotes simple excess in quantity, at another point unfairness.) Next, it has also been claimed that the unjust man is wise and good. He will, then, resemble others who are wise and good, and the just man will not. Each will be 'of like character with those whom he resembles' (*d* 10). This is a curious proposition. It is evidently untrue that things alike in one respect are alike in all. Yet unless this meant, the argument falls to the ground. On the second stage, see 349 *e* 1 n.

b 2 τοῦ δικαίου is masculine. The *action* of a just man is the subject of the next question (*b* 6).

b 4 ἀστεῖος 'well-bred ', 'gentlemanly,' like the Latin *urbanus*.

b 11 τοῦ μὲν δικαίου . . . τοῦ δ' ἀδίκου : here the ambiguity of πλέον ἔχειν appears. The just man tries to *surpass* the unjust man, but he does not claim a bigger share (though Thras. probably supposes that he would), *d* 3 δέ γε : See 346 *c* 9 n.

d 8 τοιοῦτος generalizes the statement : 'surely a man with a certain quality must resemble others who have that quality.'

d 9 ὁ δὲ μὴ ἐοικέναι. Some mss. add a second μή, but it is not needed. 'Ο δέ, ' the other,' indicates the person who is μὴ τοιοῦτος.

d 10 οἷσπερ : We should understand οἷοι ἐκεῖνοι : 'each has the quality of those whom he resembles.'

d 12 ἀλλὰ τί μέλλει ; 'what else ? ' a formula of assent, with some surprise at the question.

e 1 μουσικὸν δέ τινα, etc. Here begins a second stage in the argument. In music and in medicine, the skilled man would not try to 'surpass' the limit set by another skilled man, and expressed in his action. One cannot tune a lyre which is already in tune. But he would wish to surpass, or do better than, the non-skilled man. This is true of knowledge and ignorance in all branches (ἐπιστήμη, ἀνεπιστη-μοσύνη). But (*b* 3) the ἐπιστήμων is wise and good. Thus it is clear from the examples just shown that a wise and good man is retrained. But the characteristic here ascribed to the wise and good man was ascribed, in the earlier half of this argument, to the just man. And the just man 'is like those whom he resembles,' i.e. is wise and good.

e 7 ἅπερ . . . ἃ δε, accusatives of respect, 'good where he is wise, and bad where he is ignorant.'

350 a 1 ἐν τῇ ἐδωδῇ ἢ πόσει : The Greek rule for diet, as well as for other things in the sphere of health, (such as exercise) was that it should be neither too much nor too little. The physicians supported the plain man's view and declared that there were certain opposites which the body required in due proportion—the hot, the cold, the dry, the moist. Hence there was an obvious analogy between physical health, and harmony in music.

Socrates' argument is that the unskilled person, being unaware of the existence of a limit, and never recognizing that the mean had already been reached, would constantly fall into error on one side or the other.

a 9 τῷ ὁμοίῳ ἑαυτῷ, 'one who is like (to) himself.'

b 14 ἡμῖν 'we find that . . .'—ethic dative.

c 10 ἀναπέφανται 'is revealed as'. Cf. 334 a 10.

c 12 δή, the reading of F, seems to have more point here than δέ, that of A. δή is the usual particle in a summary : 'Thrasymachus, then, admitted all these points.'

d 1 οὐχ . . . λέγω. 'The antecedent (i.e. ῥᾳδίως) is idiomatically attracted into the relative clause' (Adam).

d 7 ἰσχυρόν: For the neuter, cf. 344 c 5, 345 a 4, 351 a 3.

e 2 ταῖς γραυσίν : Cf. γραῶν ὕθλος, Theaet. 176 b ; τάχα δ'οὖν ταῦτα μῦθός σοι δοκεῖ λέγεσθαι, ὥσπερ γραός, Gorgias 527 a.

e 4 κατανεύσομαι, ἀνανεύσομαι : compounds of νεύω, 'nod,' having a middle form, but an active sense, Cf. 351 c. For the prepositions cf. κατάφασις 'assertion' and ἀπόφασις 'denial'.

351 a 7 οὕτως ἁπλῶς 'in this simple fashion '—i.e. without the necessary distinctions and qualifications.

b 1 πόλιν φαίης ἄν, etc. 'You would agree that it was unjust for a city . . .' There is a double accusative and infinitive construction, ἄδικον εἶναι depending on φαίης and πόλιν ἐπιχειρεῖν on ἄδικον. The καί before ἄλλας is 'both'. Hence three stages in conquest are distinguished—the attempt, the successful enslavement (καταδεδουλῶσθαι), and the permanent subjection of those conquered.

b 6 Μανθάνω, ἔφην, ὅτι . . . 'I realize that . . .' Cf. 352 d 1.

c 10 ἔθνος : not 'nation ', as at 348 d 6, but 'class '.

d 9 ἔργον, 'result.' This word is not yet used in the special sense given to it in 352 d ff., 'a function.'

d 10 ἐλευθέροις τε καὶ δούλοις. 'Plato wishes to emphasize the universality of the rule, and that is why he specifies the two classes into which society is divided ' (Adam). There may also be a more definite point. In considering questions of conduct, the Greeks normally neglected slaves, as being incapable of ἀρετή. Plato shows that even among them injustice must produce its ill effects.

As we see later in the *Republic*, Justice in the State, i.e. in the relation of men to each other, is only a reflection of a harmony within the soul. In the soul there is a faculty born to command—reason—and two others born to obey, the passions associated with spirit (θυμός) and those associated with desire (ἐπιθυμία). Σωφροσύνη (self-control) is the subjection of the passions to their natural superior, and Justice the devotion of each of the three faculties to its proper function. It is therefore the function of virtue to unify the soul, and of vice to divide it—but Plato knows that such unity is not attainable without a constant struggle. Thus he says in the *Laws* (Book I) that not only is city always at war with city and man with man, but each man with himself.

e 8 μῶν μὴ ἀπολεῖ : μῶν is used to introduce a surprised question, expecting a negative answer. μή is intended to strengthen the negative force, not to remove it : ' surely it will never lose . . .'

352 a 2 ποιεῖν depends on οἵαν in 351 *e* 12, ' such as to make it unable to act . . .' The reading of the best mss., ποιεῖ, is impossible.

b 1 Καὶ θεοῖς ἄρα ἐχθρός : As he is hated by the Gods, he will be liable to all the hindrances and punishments which depend on them. In common speech θεοῖς ἐχθρός meant ' loathsome,' ' contemptible '.

b 3 Plato is particularly fond of this comparison of discussion to a feast.

b 6 ὅτι μὲν γὰρ etc. A winding but quite lucid sentence. The speaker opens with a ' that . . . ' clause, with no definite main verb in view. The remark that unjust men cannot act together leads to a parenthesis (ἀλλὰ δὴ etc.) showing that unjust men may seem to have collaborated, but only through some remnant of justice. The original ' that ' is then resumed (*d* 1, ταῦτα μὲν οὖν).

b 8 οὐδὲ πράττειν, ' not to act at all.' Cf. 329 *a* 9 οὐδὲ ζῶντες. Some mss. read οὐδέν.

c 5 μήτοι . . . ἀδικεῖν, ' at least not to practise injustice upon each other, whilst they were attacking their victims.' ἦσαν here is the imperfect of εἶμι, I go.

e 7 ἀκούσαις : We must supply ἔσθ' ὅτῳ ἂν from the last question.

e 9 I bracket ἄν, with Adam and Burnet. If it is retained, ἄν must go with εἶναι, ' we are right in saying that there would be.'

353 a 5 ἐργασθέντι ' manufactured '.

— τούτῳ : this dative, like that at 341 *e* 7, expresses purpose : but the right reading may be τοῦτο.

a 8 μὲν οὖν : see 341 *a* 9 n.

a 10 ὃ ἄν, etc. The subject of the clause is τι, ' whatever a thing performs . . .'

a 11 κάλλιστα τῶν ἄλλων. An idiom which seems to have arisen by a blend of κάλλιστα πάντων with κάλλιον τῶν ἄλλων.

b 8 ἦν : an allusion to 352 **e** 9.

c 1 ἀπεργάσαιντο. Why plural? Perhaps because Plato's thought passes from the neuter ὄμματα to the masc. ὀφθαλμοί. See Adam's note for an analysis of some similar instances in Plato.

c 1–2 οἰκείαν ἀρετὴν . . . κακίαν : Here it is the former notion which is essential, but in X 608 (one of Plato's proofs of the immortality of the soul) it is the latter. Not blindness, but ὀφθαλμία is there said to be the κακία of the eyes.

c 5 ἥτις, ' whatever.'

c 6 τῇ οἰκείᾳ μὲν ἀρετῇ. The same sense would be better conveyed by ἀρετῇ μὲν τῇ οἰκείᾳ, etc. It would then be clear that οἰκεία went with both ἀρετή and κακία. But we must beware of trying to improve upon Plato's order. After all, his concern in this argument is with the ἀρετή alone, and this would justify him in attaching the epithet to it.

d 7 ἀποδοῖμεν, ' assign.' ἀποδιδόναι is to render what is due : cf. its use in the first argument 332 a ff.

d 10 Τί δ' αὖ τὸ ζῆν; ' Soul ' is the most usual translation of ψυχή, but in fact it has some of the associations of ' mind ', and some of those of ' life '. ψυχή is the principle of life, common to plants, animals, men and the Gods themselves ; all things living are ἔμψυχα. But there are many degrees of ψυχή—plants only show their life by growth, nourishment and reproduction, animals also by movement and sensation ; men in both these ways, and also by intelligence and thought. This division, taken from Aristotle, corresponds closely to the ordinary Greek view. It was a view which stressed the continuity between all the degrees of ψυχή, and regarded man not as a separate being, but as the highest of the animals. Christianity is probably responsible for our different use of the word ' soul ', for it tends to contrast human nature with the rest of creation, and to single out certain elements within human nature as valuable. But Plato—in this respect not a typical Greek—had led the way. For him also the great difference lies between man, who is rational and can discover his place in the cosmos, enjoying the order and symmetry which prevail in it, and the unintelligent beings which blindly fulfil their function.

Ψυχή, then, is the soul as a source of life. Even so the present argument seems fallacious. Plato says that if ψυχή enables a man to live, ἀρετή of soul enables him to live well, εὖ ζῆν. But ' live well ' is ambiguous. If ψυχή is life, the correct conclusion seems to be that ἀρετή of soul provides abundance of life, or its excellence on a merely animal plane.

The phrase εὖ ζῆν, however, indicates not abundance of life, but qualitative superiority—it is used in a moral sense, to which there can be no possible transition from the sense of ψυχή as ' life '. (Cf. the complaint of Cephalus' friends, τότε μὲν εὖ ζῶντες, νῦν δὲ οὐδὲ ζῶντες:)

e 7 συνεχωρήσαμεν. This has not been formally admitted, but perhaps the reference is to 350 *d*, διωμολογησάμεθα τὴν δικαιοσύνην ἀρετὴν εἶναι καὶ σοφίαν, τὴν δὲ ἀδικίαν κακίαν τε καὶ ἀμαθίαν. Cf. also 335 *c*.

354 a 1 ὅ γε εὖ ζῶν μακάριος etc.
Plato here makes no subtle distinction between happiness and pleasure, and he does not specify exactly the *kind* of enjoyment which would accompany virtue. μακάριος ' enviable ' or ' divinely happy ', suggests pleasure, but of a more lasting kind than ἡδονή.

a 12 Βενδιδίοις. See 327 *a* 2 n.

a 13 ὑπὸ σοῦ γε, ' thanks to you.'

b 2 τοῦ . . . ἁρπάζοντες, ' they grab a sample of every dish as it is carried round.'

b 7 ἐμπεσόντος αὖ ὕστερον : On this view of the argument, see 343 *b* 5 n.

b 9 τὸ μὴ οὐκ . . . ἐλθεῖν. Many verbs expressing hindrance or restraint are followed by μή with the infinitive. If they themselves are negative, they are followed by the double negative μή οὐ.

APPENDIX

330D 7. οἵ τε γὰρ λεγόμενοι μῦθοι περὶ τῶν ἐν Ἅιδου, ὡς τὸν ἐνθάδε ἀδικήσαντα δεῖ ἐκεῖ διδόναι δίκην, καταγελώμενοι τέως, τότε δὴ στρέφουσιν αὐτοῦ τὴν ψυχὴν μὴ ἀληθεῖς ὦσιν.

The legends to which Cephalus here refers do not merely describe the fate of the human soul in Hades, but threaten the unjust man with punishment for the crimes he has committed on earth. Where are such legends to be found in Greek mythology?

A speech made by Adeimantus in the next book of the *Republic* (363A foll.) is the best commentary on the present passage, for it shows what the legends were, and what doubts occurred to an intelligent man. He says that we seldom or never hear Justice recommended for its own sake ; we generally hear that it is advantageous and brings worldly prosperity. Homer and Hesiod come under this condemnation : on behalf of the Gods they promise all kinds of blessings—in the present life, it should be noticed—to the just man : his trees shall be laden with fruit, his sheep clothed with rich fleeces, and so on. Even more stupendous are the rewards which ' Musaeus and his son ' promise to the just—for they take them to Hades, place garlands on their heads, and bring them to a place where an everlasting symposium is prepared for the devout. Some carry on the tale of recompense into future generations ; they promise that the pious man, who is faithful to the pledged word, shall become the parent of a thriving race. But the impious and unjust (τοὺς δὲ ἀνοσίους αὖ καὶ ἀδίκους) they immerse in mud somewhere else in the underworld, and make them carry water in a sieve ; and they promise them an evil reputation in their lifetime.

111

Notice especially two points (1) the underworld of Homer and Hesiod is not a place where the unjust are punished, and so is not mentioned here by Adeimantus, (2) ' Musaeus and his son '—i.e. Eumolpus—are responsible for the legends about the punishment of the guilty : now these were the reputed authors of poems, which survive only in fragments, containing the doctrines of the *Orphic* religion.   It was from this and other ' new ' religions that the Greeks obtained, not indeed their belief that the soul survives the body (for that belief is also presupposed in Homer), but the hope that under certain conditions their souls might pass on to a blessed existence, more desirable even than the life on earth.   I mention the Orphic beliefs, partly because their influence is definitely traceable in Plato, and partly because Orphic belief about the future life was expressed *in literary form*.   The appeal of the Eleusinian mysteries came from the same source, and was probably more universal ;   but here no doctrine was taught, either in a direct or in a symbolic form ;   no renunciation of the world and its pleasures was expected from the initiates.   The mysteries consisted of a pageant, τὰ δρώμενα, unaccompanied, as far as we can tell, by any spoken or written interpretation.

The statement that the underworld of Homer is not a place of punishment for the guilty needs some justification. Homer, as may be seen from some passages which Plato selects for criticism in Book III, paints a gloomy enough picture of ' the house of Hades '.   Achilles would rather be the servant of a toiling peasant on earth than king of all the shades below. The dwelling of Hades is loathsome to the Gods themselves ;   it is a dark place beneath the earth, where the feeble and unintelligent souls cluster like bats in a cavern.   Odysseus, in his visit to Hades (*Odyssey* XI) not only talks to the shades of those whom he had known, and asks for information about his voyage from Teiresias, but also witnesses a few classic punishments, such as those of Sisyphus and Tantalus.   But observe here (1) that this general impression of gloom is something different from the representation of Hades as a place of judgment.   Homer and Hesiod believe that this futile life, in a place where the sun never shines, is *the inevitable destiny* of the soul, unless—as in the case of a few great heroes—a man is transported to the Isles of the Blest, where he survives as a living person, a human being with a real body. (2) The eleventh book of the *Odyssey* invites comparison with the journeys to Hades in the epics of Vergil and Dante, but really differs from them exactly in the point which we have under review : it should be viewed as a necessary stage in the development of the drama of the *Odyssey*, not as an essay in infernal topography, designed to frighten wrongdoers. Odysseus goes to Hades partly to get practical information from Teiresias, partly to see his mother and to exchange news with the shades of those whom he had known at Troy. And he does not pass through the house of Hades, but remains standing at the fringe, and calls up the shades to drink from a trench filled with blood. Hence it is likely that the passage which makes him witness the punishment of Tantalus and Sisyphus is a later interpolation ; it is inconsistent with the original situation in the book. (3) These unfortunate victims are punished, not for an unjust life, but for a direct offence against particular Gods. There is no mention of a judgment passed on the deeds of earthly life. Minos indeed sits apart as a judge, but a judge of disputes which arise in Hades ($\theta\epsilon\mu\iota\sigma\tau\epsilon\acute{\upsilon}o\nu\tau\alpha$ $\nu\acute{\epsilon}\kappa\upsilon\sigma\sigma\iota\nu$) ; whereas, in Plato's myth at the end of the *Gorgias*, he and Rhadamanthus are the judges before whom a man's past life is reviewed.

Obviously it must not be supposed that the ' new ' religions—the cults of Demeter and Persephone, Dionysus, and Orpheus—instantly transformed Greek feeling and began to give a refined and spiritual picture of the future life. (1) As Adeimantus can bear witness, the Orphic religion, though it apparently enjoined abstinence in earthly life, continued to promise a gross and physical compensation in the next world. Even here, however, we may say in its favour that its conception of future punishment was not a cruel or vindictive one, and did not serve as a pattern to the medieval imagination. (2) Rewards were promised in the first instance to the ὅσιοι, i.e. the pure or initiated, and only in a secondary way to the δίκαιοι. (This comes out in the speech of Adeimantus, cf. 363 C 5 συμπόσιον τῶν ὁσίων; D 4 τοῦ ὁσίου καὶ εὐόρκου; D 5 τοὺς δὲ ἀνοσίους αὖ καὶ ἀδίκους.)   Now the notion of ὁσιότης is sometimes explained as the performance of what is due to the Gods, just as δικαιοσύνη is the rendering of what is owed to men.   But it should not be overlooked that the demands of ὁσιότης may be in flagrant contrast with those of ethics.   We see this in many of the legends used by the tragedians. Certain actions involve a pollution or impurity, which inevitably brings divine displeasure in its train.   Under this displeasure the innocent suffer alike with the guilty, as though by some blind natural causation, until the source of pollution is removed.   Such a view may do credit to the scientific sense of the Greeks, but it is not a sign of a highly developed *ethical* sense.   The point at issue is well put in a remark attributed to Diogenes the Cynic, who lived in the time of Alexander : ' Will Pataikion the thief, because he has been initiated at Eleusis, enjoy a better fate in the next life than Agesilaus or Epameinondas ? '

Let us conclude with a brief survey of Plato's religion, and his belief about the soul.   Neither man himself nor the world which he studies is entirely rational, and we are bound to believe much which we cannot strictly demonstrate to be true.   In the *Phaedo* Plato proves that the soul as the source of reason and understanding, in which the eternal Ideas are reflected, must be exempt from change and corruption.   In later Dialogues he shows that ψυχή in general, as the principle of life throughout the universe, inspires, and so is not itself mastered by, physical change.   Neither proof implies the immortality of ψυχή as an individual human personality.   Very different are the beliefs expressed in the *myths*, where Plato, throwing off the restraint of logic, but clinging to what seems to be probable (εἰκότι μύθῳ), describes the soul's progress after death : he depicts a judgment at which Minos and

Rhadamanthus preside, then a long interval either of joy and repose, or of pain and suffering, till the time comes for the soul to make choice of a new life in human or animal shape. It is probable that Plato here borrows from the Orphic μῦθοι, but remodels them with an ethical emphasis which is his own ; at the same time he accepts the doctrine of *transmigration*, which, like the Orphic religion itself, was probably of Thracian origin, and had fascinated many of the earlier philosophers. Nor does he forget to incorporate in the myths as much of the latest physical and astronomical knowledge as may justify his claim to be giving a ' probable ' account. The religious spirit prevails more and more strongly in Plato's later philosophy. He remains tolerant of all forms of belief, and in regard to the Olympian religion would allow each citizen to think as he chooses ; but he is not tolerant of *disbelief*. The essence of religion for him is that the world in which we live is governed not by chance, but by reason and design ; and this can be proved to the satisfaction of everyone who is willing to learn mathematics and its application to the movements of the heavenly bodies ; whether the stars are merely the handiwork of the Gods, or are in literal truth visible deities, ὁρατοὶ θεοί, there is no need to inquire ; it is enough to know that the mind of God is akin to that of man, and that the world is well and wisely governed. In such a world justice and injustice will each receive their due reward, in fulfilment of the order of nature which the Gods have established and will uphold : the unjust man associates with the unjust, and must necessarily become worse (more miserable) by this contact, whereas the just man progresses in goodness and happiness.

(For fuller information see M. P. Nilsson, *A History of Greek Religion* (Oxford, Clarendon Press, 1925), chapters VI, VII, and VIII; W. K. C. Guthrie, *Orpheus and Greek Religion* (Methuen, 1953) ; and, by the same author, *The Greeks and their Gods* (Methuen, 1950), chapters X, XI, and XII.)

VOCABULARY

Note.—The gender of nouns is not given, but may usually be inferred from their formation. It will be helpful to learn from elsewhere the principal parts of the chief verbs.

ἀβλαβής, *adj.*, unharmed, unimpaired.

ἀγαθός, *adj.*, good.

ἄγαμαι, *v.tr.* (*aor.* ἀγασθῆναι), wonder at

ἀγανακτῶ, *v.intr.*, be vexed (with)

ἀγαπῶ, *v.tr.*, love : *v.intr.*, be content

ἀγνοῶ, *v.tr.* or *intr.*, be ignorant

ἄγριος, *adj.*, fierce

ἄγω, *v.tr.*, lead : ἑορτήν ἀ., hold : ἡσυχίαν ἀ., keep quiet

ἀδελφός, *n.*, brother

ἄδην, *adv.*, enough

ἀδίκημα, *n.*, unjust act

ἀδικία, *n.*, injustice

ἄδικος, *adj.*, unjust : *adv.*, -ως

ἀδικῶ, *v.intr.*, be unjust

ἀδύνατος, *adj.*, impossible, unable

ἀεί, *adv.*, always

ἄθλιος, *adj.*, unfortunate, miserable

ἀθρόος, *adj.*, abundant, copious

αἰνίττομαι, *v.intr.*, speak in riddles

αἱροῦμαι, *v.tr.*, choose

αἰσχρός, *adj.*, ugly, dishonourable

αἴτιος, *adj.*, responsible : τὸ ἀ., the cause

αἰτιῶμαι, *v.tr.*, accuse, blame

αἰτῶ, *v.tr.*, ask for

ἀκέραιος, *adj.*, whole, unimpaired

ἀκοή, *n.*, power of hearing

ἀκολουθῶ, *v.tr.*, follow ; abide by

ἀκούω, *v.tr.*, hear

ἀκριβής, *adj.*, accurate (*adv.* -βῶς)

ἀκριβολογοῦμαι, *v.intr.*, consider accurately

ἄκων, *adj.*, unwilling

ἀλήθεια, *n.*, truth

ἀληθής, *adj.*, true : ὡς ἀληθῶς, in truth

ἀληθινός, *adj.*, true, genuine

ἀλλά, *conj.*, but

ἀλλήλων, *dat.* -οις, *pron.*, each other

ἄλλος, *adj.*, other : ἄλλο τι, in interrogation, *is it not true* . . .

ἀλλότριος, *adj.*, another's

ἅμα, *adv.*, at the same time

ἀμαθής, *adj.*, ignorant : ἀμαθία, *n.*, ignorance

ἀμείνων, *adj.*, *compar. of* ἀγαθός, better

ἀμέλεια, *n.*, neglect

ἀμιλλῶμαι, *v.intr.*, strive, compete

ἄμουσος, *adj.*, unmusical

ἄμπελος, *n.*, vine : -πελουργικὴ sc. τέχνη, culture of the vine

ἄν, *conj.* = ἐάν, if

ἄν, *particle* indicating a condition, whether expressed or latent. See 352 E, n., ὃς ἄν with subj. = whoever.

ἀνά, *prep. c.acc.*, up, towards ; (in distributions) according to

ἀνά, compounds of—

— καγχάζω, *intr.*, laugh, cackle

— λογίζομαι, *tr.*, consider, compute

— μιμνήσκω, *tr.*, remind

— νεύω, *tr.*, reject, say no

— ὁμολογοῦμαι, *intr.*, make an agreement

— ὀρθῶ, *tr.*, rectify

— φαίνω, *tr.*, reveal

ἀναγκάζω, *v.tr.*, compel

117

ἀνάγκη, *n.*, necessity : *adj.*,
ἀναγκαῖος, compulsory
ἀναμάρτητος, *adj.*, unerring
ἀνδραποδίζομαι, *v.tr.*, kidnap, enslave : *n.*, -ποδιστής, kid-
napper
ἀνεπιστημοσύνη, *n.*, want of knowledge : *adj.*, -μων, without
knowledge
ἄνεσις, *n.*, relaxation
ἄνευ, *prep.*, without
ἀνήρ, ἀνδρός, *n.*, man
ἀνθρώπειος, *adj.*, human
ἀντί, *prep.*, instead of, in exchange
for
ἀντικατατείνω, *v.intr.*, contend
with
—— λαμβάνομαι, *v.tr.*, lay hold
upon (*c.gen.*)
ἄξιος, *adj.*, deserving, worthy
ἀξιῶ, *v.tr.*, claim
ἅπας, *adj.*, all, every
ἀπέραντος, *adj.*, unending
ἀπιστῶ, *v.intr.*, distrust, disbelieve
ἁπλῶς, *adv.*, simply, absolutely
ἀπό, *prep.*, from ; owing to
ἀπο, compounds of—
    ἀπαιτῶ, *tr.*, demand in return
    —αλλάττομαι, *intr.*, escape from,
    abandon (*perf.*, ἀπηλλάχ-
    θαι)
    — ειμι, *intr.*, go away
    — εἶπον, *perf. part.* ἀπειρημένον,
    forbid
    — ἐργάζομαι, *tr.*, achieve
    — ἔχομαι, *intr.*, abstain or
    withdraw from
    — οκνῶ, *intr.*, shrink from
    — ὄλλυμι, *tr.*, spoil, destroy,
    lose
ἀπογεύομαι, *tr.*, taste
    — δέχομαι, *tr.*, accept, admit
    — δίδωμι, *tr.*, restore : δίδομαι,
    sell
    — κρίνομαι, *intr.*, answer
    — λαμβάνω, *tr.*, receive
    — λαύω, *tr.* or *intr.*, profit by
    — μαραίνομαι, *intr.*, fade away

    — μύττω, *tr.*, wipe the nose
    — πληρῶ, *tr.*, satisfy
    — στερῶ, *tr.*, deprive
    — τέμνω, *tr.*, cut off
    — τίνω, *tr.*, pay back
    — φαίνω, *tr.*, prove
    — φεύγω, *tr.*, escape from
ἀφαιρῶ, *tr.*, take away from
    — ἵημι, *tr.*, dismiss, let go
ἀπόδοσις, *n.*, restoration
ἀποστερητής, *n.*, robber
ἀπόκρισις, *n.*, answer
ἄρα, *part.*, therefore, apparently
ἆρα, *interrog. particle* ; ἆρ' οὐ =
Latin *nonne*
ἀργύριον, *n.*, silver ; money
ἀρετή, *n.*, virtue
ἀριθμῶ, *v.tr.*, count
ἄριστος, *adj.*, *superl. of* ἀγαθός,
excellent, best
ἁρμόττω, *v.tr.*, harmonize, adapt :
-όττομαι, tune an instrument
ἄρνυμαι, *v.tr.*, earn, acquire
ἁρπάζω, *v.tr.*, seize, snatch
ἄρτι, *adv.*, just now
ἀρχή, *n.*, beginning ;   office,
place of authority
ἄρχω, *v.intr.*, rule over ; begin
ἀσθένεια, *n.*, weakness
ἄσμενος, *adj.*, glad : *adv.*, ἀσμενέστατα, most gladly
ἀσπάζομαι, *v.tr.*, welcome
ἀσπίς, *n.*, shield
ἀστεῖος, *adj.*, civilized, charming
ἄστυ, *n.*, city
ἀσύμφορος, *adj.*, disadvantageous
ἀτάλλω, *v.tr.*, refresh (Pindar)
ἀτεχνῶς, *adv.*, simply, exactly
ἅτε, *adv.* (usu. with genitive
absolute), inasmuch as
ἄττα = τινά, certain things
αὖ, *adv.*, again ; on the contrary
αὖθις, *adv.*, again
αὔξω, *v.tr.*, increase
αὐτίκα, *adv.*, immediately ;   for
instance
αὐτόθι, *adv.*, there
αὐτός, ή, όν, *pronoun*, he, she, it

ἀφαιρῶ, ἀφίημι, *see* compounds of ἀπό

ἄφιππος, *adj.*, unskilful with horses

ἀφροδίσια, τά, *n.*, love affairs

ἄφρων, *adj.*, foolish

ἄφωνος, *adj.*, speechless

ἄχρηστος, *adj.*, useless (ἀχρηστία, disuse)

βαλανεύς, *n.*, bath attendant

βαλλάντιον, *n.*, purse

βδελυρός, *adj.*, offensive, disgusting

βέβαιος, *adj.*, firm

βελτίων, βέλτιστος, *compar. and superl. of* ἀγαθός, better, best

βία, *n.*, violence

βιάζομαι, *v.tr.*, do violence to

βίος, *n.*, life

βιώσομαι, *v.intr.*, will live

βλάβη, *n.*, harm, injury

βλάπτω, *v.tr.*, harm, injure

βλέπω, *v.intr.*, look

βούλευμα, *n.*, scheme

βουλεύομαι, *v.intr.*, consider, make plans

βούλομαι, *v.tr.*, wish

βοῦς, βοός, *n.*, ox

βραχύς, εῖα, ύ, *adj.*, small, slight

γάρ, *conj.*, for

γε, *part.*, at least, indeed

γελῶ, *aor.* ἐγέλασα, laugh

γενναῖος, *adj.*, noble ; excellent

γένος, *n.*, kind, class

γέρων, *n.*, old man

γεωργία, *n.*, agriculture

γῆρας, *n.*, old age : -ότροφος, *adj.*, nurse of old age (Pindar)

γίγνομαι, *v.intr.*, become

γιγνώσκω, *v.tr.*, know

γλυκύς, εῖα, ύ, *adj.*, sweet

γνώριμος, *adj.*, known : ὁ γ., an acquaintance

γοῦν, *part.*, certainly

γραμματιστής, *n.*, writing-master

γραῦς, γραός, *n.*, old woman

γυνή, -αικός, *n.*, woman

δαιμόνιος, *adj.*, god-like; admirable

δαιτυμών, *n.*, guest, banqueter

δέ, *part.*, but : δέ γε, *see* 346 c 9, *n.*

δεῖ, *v.intr.* and *impers.*, one ought ; one needs

δείκνυμι, *v.tr.*, show

δεῖμα, *n.*, fear : δειμαίνω, *v.intr.*, be afraid

δεινός, *adj.*, clever ; dangerous, terrible

δεῖπνον, *n.*, dinner

δέος, *n.*, fear

δεσπότης, *n.*, master, owner (*adj.*, -οτικός)

δεῦρο, *adv.*, hither

δή, *part.*, indeed ; therefore : δῆτα, certainly

δῆλος, *adj.*, clear

δημηγορῶ, *v.intr.*, make an oration

δημιουργός, *n.*, craftsman

δημιουργῶ, *v.tr. or intr.*, work as a craftsman

δημοκρατοῦμαι, *v.tr.*, be ruled democratically

δημόσιος, *adj.*, public (*adv.*, δημοσίᾳ)

Δία, *accus. of* Ζεύς

διά, *prep. c.gen.*, through : *c.acc.*, owing to

διά, compounds of—

— ἄγω, *tr.*, pass through, spend (time)

— ἀκούω, *tr.*, hear to the end

— ἁμαρτάνω, *tr.*, be quite mistaken in (τινός)

— ἁρπάζω, *tr.*, tear to pieces

— ἔρχομαι, *tr.*, traverse, describe

— ὁρίζω, *tr.*, define

— δίδωμι, *tr.*, pass on to another

— κρίνω, *tr.*, distinguish, decide

— κωλύω, *tr.*, prevent

διά λέγομαι, *intr.*, converse (τινί)
— μάχομαι, *intr.*, strive, succeed by force
— νοοῦμαι, *tr.*, think, reflect
— παύω, *tr.*, check ; (*mid.*) cease
— πράττω, *tr.*, achieve
— πτοῶ, *tr.*, scare
— σκέπτομαι (*aor.* σκέψασθαι), inquire
— σώζω, *tr.*, preserve
— τίθημι, *tr.*, dispose, arrange
— φέρω (*fut. mid.* διοίσομαι) differ ; quarrel with
— φθείρω, *tr.*, spoil, destroy
Διαγωγή, *n.*, way of spending (time)
διάλογος, *n.*, dialogue
διάλυσις, *n.*, dissolution
διδάσκω, *v.tr.*, teach
δίδωμι, *v.tr.*, give
δίκαιος, *adj.*, just
δικαιοσύνη, *n.*, justice
δικαστής, *n.*, judge
δίκη, *n.*, judgment : δ. διδόναι, be punished
διπλῆ, *adv.*, twice **as much**
δίς, *adv.*, twice
δίφρος, *n.*, chair
δοκῶ, *v.tr.*, think : **seem**
δόξα, *n.*, opinion, expectation
δοξάζω, *v.tr.* or *intr.*, judge
δουλῶ, *v.tr.*, enslave
δραμόντα, *see* τρέχειν
δρέπανον, *n.*, sickle
δρῶ, *v.tr.*, do, act
δύναμαι, *v.tr.*, be able
δύναμις, *n.*, power, faculty
δυνατός, *adj.*, able : δυνατόν, possible
δώδεκα (*numeral*), twelve

ἑ, *reflexive pronoun, accus. of* ὅς, himself
ἐάν, *conj.*, if (followed by subjunctive)
ἑαυτοῦ, *reflex. pronoun*, oneself

ἐγγίγνομαι (*aor.* ἐγγενέσθαι), *v.intr.*, appear in
ἐγγύς, *adv.*, near (*compar.* ἐγγυτέρω)
ἐγείρω, *v.tr.*, rouse : *mid.*, wake up
ἐγώ, *pronoun*, I
ἐδωδή, *n.*, eating
ἐθέλω, *v.intr.*, be willing, consent
ἔθνος, *n.*, nation (*opp. to* πόλις) ; class, kind
εἰ, *conj.*, if
εἴασα, *aor. of* ἐῶ, *q.v.*
εἶδον, *v.tr.*, saw (*used as aor. of* ὁρῶ)
εἶεν, *connecting particle*, agreed, well then
εἴκω, *v.intr.*, yield : *aor.* (1) εἶκα, resemble ; hence εἰκός, probable, likely : (2) οἶκα or ἔοικα, be probable, be like
εἰμί, *v.intr.*, am : *future* ἔσομαι, *imperf.* ἦν, *pres. part.* ὤν, οὖσα, ὄν, *pres. subj.* ὦ : τὸ ὄν, the truth, reality
εἶμι, *v.intr.*, go : *infin.* ἰέναι, *pres. part.* ἰών, ἰοῦσα, *imperf.* ἦν (*third pers. sing.* ᾔει, *plur.* ᾖσαν) ; *imper.* ἴθι : ἴθι δή, come now
εἶπον, *v.tr.*, said
εἴρηκα, *v.tr.*, have said
εἰρήνη, *n.*, peace
εἰρώνεια, (*n.*,) self-disparagement (*v.intr.*, εἰρωνεύομαι)
εἰς, *prep.*, to, towards, in respect of
εἷς, μία, ἕν (*numeral*), one
εἰς, compounds of—
— εἶμι, *whence part.* εἰσίων, go in
— ἔρχομαι, *whence aor.* εἰσῆλθον, go in
— φέρω, *tr.*, contribute
εἰσαῦθις, *adv.*, at a later time
εἰσοίσω, *future of* εἰσφέρω
εἴσομαι, *future of* οἶδα
εἰσφορά, *n.*, contribution
εἰωθώς, -υῖα, -ός (*part. of* εἴωθα, be wont), customary
εἶτα, *adv.*, then, next

εἴτε . . . εἴτε, whether . . . or,
Latin *sive* . . . *sive*
ἐκ, *prep.*, from, out of
ἐκ or ἐξ, compounds of—
ἐκβαίνω, *intr.*, depart from
— πλήττω, *tr.* (*aor. pass.*
ἐξεπλάγην*), terrify
— πορίζω, *tr.*, devise
— τίνω, *tr.*, pay
ἐξαγγέλλω, *tr.*, report on
— ἀγριαίνω, *tr.*, infuriate
— ἁμαρτάνω, *intr.*, go astray
— ἀνίστημι, *intr.*, get up and
go out
— ἀπατῶ, *tr.*, deceive
— ἀρκῶ, *intr.*, suffice
— εὑρίσκω, *tr.*, find out, invent
ἕκαστος, *adj.*, each, every (-άστοτε,
always)
ἑκάτερος, *adj.*, each of two
ἐκεῖ, *adv.*, there
ἐκεῖνος, η, ο, *demonstr. pron.*, that
ἑκών, *adj.*, willing
ἐλάττων, *adj.*, less, smaller
ἐλάχιστος, *adj.*, least, smallest
ἐλέγχω, *v.tr.*, examine ; refute
ἐλευθέριος, *adj.*, liberal, generous
ἐλεύθερος, *adj.*, free
ἐλεῶ, *v.tr.*, pity
ἕλκω, *v.tr.*, drag
ἐλπίς, *n.*, hope, expectation
ἐμαυτοῦ, *pron.*, myself
ἐμός, *adj. of* ἐγώ, my
ἔμπροσθεν, *adv.*, previously
ἐν, *prep.*, in : ἐν ᾧ, whilst
ἐν, compounds of—
ἐμβάλλω, *tr.*, throw among
— μένω, *intr.*, abide by (τινί)
— πίπτω, *intr.*, fall into :
ἐμπεσών, occurring
— ποιῶ, *tr.*, inflict
ἐνδείκνυμι, *tr.*, display, prove
— ειμι, *intr.*, be within
— νοῶ, *tr.*, consider
— τίθημι, *tr.*, put into
— τυγχάνω, *tr.*, meet with
ἐναντίος, *adj.*, opposite, reverse
ἐναντιοῦμαι, *v.intr.*, oppose (τινί)

ἔνδον, *adv.*, within, indoors
ἕνεκα, for the sake of : ἕνεκα . . .
γήρως, as far as old age is
concerned
ἐνθάδε, *adv.*, hither, here
ἔνιοι, some : *adv.*, ἐνίοτε, sometimes
ἐνταῦθα, *adv.*, there ; (*c.gen.*),
so far advanced in . . .
ἕξ (*numeral*), six
ἐξ, compounds of, see ἐκ
ἑξῆς, *adv.*, in succession ; ὁ ἐ,
the next
ἑορτή, *n.*, festival
ἐπεί, *conj.*, when ; since
ἐπειδάν, *conj.*, whenever : (*with
aor. subj.*), after
ἐπειδή, *conj.*, since ; after
ἔπειτα, *adv.*, next ; after all
ἐπί, *preposition c.dat.*, upon, with
a view to, on account of :
c.acc., towards
ἐπί, compounds of—
ἐπαινῶ, *tr.*, praise
— εξέρχομαι, *intr.*, pursue (*aor.*
ἐπεξελθεῖν)
ἐπικτῶμαι, *tr.*, earn in addition
— λείπω, *intr.*, be finished
— μελοῦμαι, *tr.*, supervise
(τινός)
— νεύω, *tr.* or *intr.*, agree to
— τάττω, *tr.*, instruct, command
— τρέπω, *tr.*, entrust
— χειρῶ, *intr.*, attempt (τινί)
ἐπιβουλή, *n.*, plot, conspiracy
ἐπιεικής, *adj.*, decent, respectable
ἐπιθυμία, *n.*, desire
ἐπίπονος, *adj.*, laborious, painful
ἐπιστήμη, *n.*, science, knowledge
(*adj.* -μων)
ἐπίτασις, *n.*, tension, tightening
ἐπιτυχών, ὁ, *aor. of* ἐπιτυγχάνω,
casual, selected by chance
ἐπιχώριος, *adj.*, native
ἕπομαι, *v.intr.*, follow
ἐργάζομαι, *v.tr.*, work at, perform
ἔργον, *n.*, work, function

ἔρομαι, v.tr., ask
ἐρρωμένος, adj., strong ; adv. -νως
ἐρυθριῶ, v.intr., blush
ἔρχομαι (aor. ἐλθεῖν), come, proceed
ἐρωτῶ, v.tr., ask
ἑσπέρα, n., evening
ἑστίασις, n., feast
ἑστιῶ, v.tr., feast
ἑταῖρος, n., companion
ἕτερος, adj., other
ἔτι, adv., further, still
εὖ, adv., well
εὐβουλία, n., prudence
εὐδαίμων, adj., happy, fortunate
εὐδοκιμῶ, v.intr., be in good repute
εὐεργετῶ, v.tr., confer benefits
εὐήθεια, n., simplicity ;   folly (adj. -ήθης, ηθικός)
εὐηθίζομαι, v.intr., play the fool
εὐθύς, adj., straight ; (as adv.), at once, for instance
εὔκολος, adj., sweet-tempered
εὐπαθῶ, v.intr., live enjoyably
εὔπορος, adj., easily travelled
εὕρεσις, n., finding
εὑρίσκω, v.tr., find
εὐφημῶ, v.intr., speak reverently : εὐφημεῖ, imper., hush
εὐωχία, n., feast (verb, εὐωχῶ)
ἐχθρός, adj., hostile : ὁ ἐ, enemy
ἔχω, v.tr., have, hold, keep
ἐῶ, v.tr., allow
ἕως, conj., so long as ; until
ἕωσπερ, emphatic form of ἕως

ζημία, n., penalty, loss
ζημιῶ, v.tr., punish
ζητῶ, v.tr., search for : ζήτησις, n., search
ζῶ, v.intr., live
ζωή, n., life

ἤ, part., or : ἤ . . . ἤ, either . . . or

ἤ, part., surely : in questions, indicates surprise. See also ἠμί
ἡ, fem. of ὁ
ᾗ, adv., inasmuch as : distinct from ᾖ, third pers. pres. subj. of εἰμί
ἡγοῦμαι, v.tr. or intr., think, lead
ἡδέως, adv., gladly
ἤδη, adv., now, already
ἡδονή, n., pleasure
ἡδύς, εῖα, ύ, adj., pleasant, amusing
ἤδυσμα, n., seasoning, flavour
ἧκα, aor. of ἵημι
ἥκιστα, adv., least
ἥκω, v.intr., come
ἡλικία, n., age, generation
ἡμεῖς, -ᾶς, pron., we
ἡμέρα, n., day
ἠμί, obsol. form of φημί, whence imperf. ἦν, ἦ
ἡμιμόχθηρος, adj., half corrupt
ἤν (= ἐάν) conj., if
ἦν = (1) imperf. of εἰμί, was ; (2) imperf. of ἠμί, said
ἡνίκα, conj., whilst, when
ἠνίξατο, aor. of αἰνίττομαι
ἧπερ, in so far as
ἡσυχία, n., rest, quiet
ἤτοι, emphatic form of ἤ, either
ἥττων, adj., less, weaker

θάλαττα, n., sea
θαμίζω, v.intr., visit frequently (θαμά, adv.)
θαρρῶ, v.intr., be confident
θαυμάζω, v.tr. or intr., wonder (at)
θαυμάσιος ⎫ adj., wonderful
θαυμαστός ⎭ adv., θαυμαστῶς
θέα, n., spectacle
θεῖος, adj., godlike
θεός, n., god, goddess
θεραπεύω, v.tr., tend, care for (noun, -ευτής)
θερμότης, n., heat

θέρος, n., summer
θέσις, n., disposition : position (in argument)
θεῶμαι, v.tr., observe, look at
θηρίον, n., wild animal
θυσία, n., sacrifice
θύω, perf. τέθυκα, sacrifice

ἰατρική, sc. τέχνη, art of medicine
ἰατρός, n., doctor
ἴδιος, adj., private : ἰδίᾳ, privately
ἰδιωτικός, adj., private, unofficial
ἵδρως, n., sweat
ἱερός, adj., sacred : τὰ ἱερά, ceremonies
ἱερόσυλος, adj., sacrilegious person
ἵημι, v.tr., send : throw
ἴθι, see εἶμι
ἱκανός, adj., sufficient : -νῶς, on a large scale
ἱμάτιον, n., cloak
ἵνα, conj., in order that
ἵππος, n., horse : ἱππική (τέχνη) care or management of horses
ἴσος, adj., equal : adv., ἴσως, perhaps
ἰσχυρός, adj., strong
ἰῶμαι, v.tr., cure

καθέζομαι, v.intr., sit down
καθεστηκώς, -υῖα, settled, established
κάθημαι, v.intr., sit, recline
καθορῶ, καθίστημι, see κατά and compounds
καί, conj., and : καὶ δὴ καί, and especially . . .
καινός, adj., new
κακία, n., badness, viciousness
κακός, adj., bad (adv., κακῶς)
κακοήθεια, n., badness of character
κακουργῶ, v.tr., injure : -ούργημα, injury, crime
καλός, adj., fine, beautiful, honourable

καλῶ, v.tr., call, name
κάμνω, v.intr., labour, suffer
κἄν = καὶ ἄν
καρδία, n., heart
καρπός, n., fruit
κατά, prep. (1) c.accus., at (of time, place) ; in respect of, in accordance with. Also (2) c.gen., from ; against
κατά, compounds of —
καταντλῶ, tr., shower upon
καταβαίνω, intr., go down
καταγελῶ, tr., laugh at (τινός)
καταδουλοῦμαι, tr., enslave
καθίστημι, tr., establish
καταλαμβάνω, tr., discover
καταλείπω, tr., leave behind
καθορῶ (aor. κατεῖδον), observe
κατατείνω, tr., stretch : intr., strain
καταφανής, adj., manifest
κεῖμαι, v.intr., lie : of money, be invested
κέκασμαι, perf. of καίνυμαι, excel (Hom.)
κελεύω, v.tr., order
κερδαίνω, v.intr., make profit (κέρδος, n.)
κερδαλέος, adj., profitable
κήδομαι, v.tr., care for (τινός)
κιθαριστική, sc. τέχνη, art of lyre-playing
κίνδυνος, n., danger
κινδυνεύω, v.intr., run a risk : κινδυνεύει, it is likely
κινῶ, v.tr., move, incite
κλέπτης, n., thief : adj. -ικός
κλεπτοσύνη, n., thieving (Hom.)
κλέπτω, v.tr., steal, evade
κλῆμα, n., shoot, sprig
κληρονόμος, n., heir
κλητέος, adj. from καλῶ, must be called
κοινῇ, adv., jointly, in common
κοινωνία (or -ωνημα), n., partnership
κοινωνός, n., partner
κοινωνῶ, v.intr., share, take part in

κολάζω, *v.tr.*, punish
κομιδῇ, *adv.*, entirely, wholly
κορύζω, *v.intr.*, snivel
κόσμιος, *adj.*, sober, orderly
κράτιστος, *adj.*, best, excellent
κρατῶ, *v.tr.*, be stronger, be master of
κρέας (pl. κρέα), *n.*, flesh, meat
κρείττων, *adj.*, stronger, superior
κροῦμα, *n.*, striking a note, in music
κτῆσις, *n.*, acquisition ; possession
κτῶμαι, *v.tr.*, acquire : *perf.*, κέκτημαι, possess
κυβερνῶ, *v.tr.*, steer a ship
κυβερνήτης, *n.*, steersman
κύκλος, *n.*, circle
κύων (pl. κυνές), *n.*, dog

λάθρα, *adv.*, by stealth
λαμβάνω, *v.tr.*, take, receive
λαμπάδιον, *n.*, small torch
λαμπάς, *n.*, torch ; torch-race
λανθάνω, *v.tr.*, evade, elude : *v.intr.*, do unawares
λέγω, *v.tr.*, say, speak
λείπω, *v.tr.*, leave, abandon
λέων, *n.*, lion
λῃστής, *n.*, robber
λῆψις, *n.*, taking
λίθος, *n.*, stone
λίχνος, *adj.*, greedy
λογίζομαι, *v.intr.*, think, calculate
λογισμός, *n.*, calculation
λογιστικός, *adj.*, and λογιστής, *n.*, calculator
λόγος, *n.*, speech ; thought, argument, account
λοιδορῶ, *v.tr.*, abuse
λοιπός, *adj.*, remaining
λύπη, *n.*, pain
λύρα, *n.*, lyre
λυττῶ, *v.intr.*, be insane
λυσιτελῶ, *v.intr.*, be advantageous

μὰ Δία, exclamation after a negative, No, by Zeus !

μαγειρική, *sc.* τέχνη, **art of** cookery.
μαίνομαι, *aor.* μανῆναι, *v.intr.*, be mad
μακάριος, *adj.*, supremely happy
μάλα, μᾶλλον, μάλιστα, *adv.*, much (very), more (rather), most.
μανθάνω, *v.tr.* and *intr.*, learn ; understand
μαντεύομαι, *v.tr.*, prophesy, foresee
μάρτυς, *n.*, witness : -τυρῶ, bear witness
μάχαιρα, *n.*, knife
μάχη, *n.*, battle, combat
μάχομαι, *v.intr.*, fight, resist
μέγας, -άλη, *adj.*, great, important
μείζων, μέγιστος, *compar. and superl.* of μέγας
μέλει, *v.impers.*, it concerns (τινί)
μέλλω, *v.intr.*, intend ; delay
μέν, *part. announcing the first term of a contrast, and normally followed by* δέ
μέντοι, *adv.*, however
μένω, *v.intr.*, remain
μέρος, *n.*, part, portion : ἐν μισθοῦ μέρει, ranked as a reward
μέσος, *adj.*, intermediate : εἰς τὸ μ., publicly
μεστός, *adj.*, full
μετά, *prep.*, with, among
μεταστρέφομαι (*aor.* -εστράφην) turn round (*v.intr.*)
μετατίθημι, *v.tr.*, change round
μεταχειρίζομαι, *v.tr.*, take in hand, deal with
μεταξύ, *prep.*, between : see 336 b 1 n.
μετρίως, *adv.*, in moderation
μετρῶ, *v.tr.*, measure
μή, *negative particle*, not
μηδέ, nor even : μηδείς, no one μηδέποτε, never : μήτε .... μήτε, neither ... nor
μήν, *part.*, yet, however
μήτοι, *emph. form of* μή
μικρός, *adj.*, small

μιμνήσκω, v.tr., remind
μισθαρνῶ, v.intr., earn money
μισθός, n., wage, payment
μισθωτός, adj., hired : μισθωτι
κή or μισθαρνητική τέχνη,
art of making profit
μῖσος, n., hatred
μισῶ, v.tr., hate
μόγις, adv., hardly, reluctantly
μόνος, adj., alone : μόνον, only
μουσικός, adj., musical
μοχθηρός, adj., wicked, corrupt
(comp. -ότερος)
μῦθος, n., story
μῶν, interrog. particle, Lat. num,
surely not . . .

ναί, affirmative particle, yes
ναυπηγός, n., ship-builder
ναῦς, n., ship
ναύτης, n., sailor
νεανίσκος, n., youth, lad
νεότης, n., youth
νέος, adj., young
νὴ Δία = by Zeus : cf. μὰ Δία
νομιζόμενα, τὰ, n., customs, observances
νόμος, n., law, custom
νοῦς, n., mind : νοῦν ἔχων,
sensible
νοῶ, v.tr., think
νῦν, adv., now. Also νυνί
νύξ, νυκτός, n., night
νόσος, n., disease

ξηρότης, n., dryness
ξυρῶ, v.tr., shave

ὁ, ἡ, τό, def. article, the
ὅδε, ἥδε, τόδε, demonstr. pron., this
ὁδός, n., way, road
ὀδύρομαι, v.tr., bewail, deplore
ὅθεν, adv., whence
οἴκαδε, adv., to the house (of)
οἰκεῖος, adj., familiar ; closely
acquainted : (opp. ἀλλότριος)
proper, peculiar

οἰκοδομικός, adj., of building
οἴομαι (sometimes written οἶμαι),
v.tr., think
οἷος, οἵα, οἷον, rel. pron., such as ;
οἷον, as conjunction, as for
instance . . .
ὀλίγος, adj., few, slight, small
ὅλος, adj., whole
ὀλοφύρομαι, v.tr., bewail
ὄμμα, n., eye
ὅμοιος, adj., like
ὁμολογῶ, v.tr., allow, agree :
ὁμολογία, admission
ὁμόνοια, n., concord, agreement
ὁμονοῶ, v.intr., be of one mind
ὁμώνυμος, adj., called by the
same name
ὅμως, adv., nevertheless
ὀνειδίζω, v.tr., reproach, insult
ὄν, τό, see εἰμί
ὄνειδος, n., disgrace
ὄνομα, n., name
ὀνομάζω, v.tr., name, call
ὀνομαστός, adj., famous
ὅπη, in what way
ὄπισθεν, adv., behind
ὁπλιτικός, adj., of the hoplite
(heavy-armed soldier)
ὁποῖος, pron., of what kind
ὁπότε, conj., whenever
ὁποτέρως, adv., in which way
ὅπου, where
ὅπως, how ; in order that
ὁπωστιοῦν, adv., to any degree
ὀρθῶς, adv., rightly
ὁρίζομαι, v.tr., define
ὅρκος, n., oath
ὁρμῶ, v.tr., urge ; (middle) set
out, proceed
ὅρος, n., definition
ὁρῶ, v.tr., see
ὅς, ἥ, ὅ, rel. pronoun, who, which ;
ὅς may also serve as a personal
pronoun (= he), as in the phrase
ἥ δ' ὅς
ὅσιος, adj., reverent ; (of things)
sacred

ὅσος, *rel. pron.*, how great, how much, how many
ὅστις, ἥτις, ὅ τι, *pron.*, who, which
ὅταν, *conj.*, whenever
ὅτε, *conj.*, when, since
ὅτι, *conj.*, because ; that
οὐ(κ), *negative particle* : οὐδαμοῦ, nowhere : οὐδαμῇ, οὐδαμῶς, by no means : οὐδέ, nor even : οὐδείς, -δεμία, -δέν, no, none : οὐδέποτε, never : οὐδέτερος, neither : οὔτε . . . οὔτε, neither . . . nor
οὐκέτι, *adv.*, no longer
οὐκοῦν, therefore : **accented** οὔκουν, not therefore
οὐδός, *n.*, threshold
οὖν, *part.*, so, therefore
οὖς, *pl.* ὦτα, *n.*, ear
οὐσία, *n.*, being, substance ; wealth
οὗτοι, *emph. form of* οὐ, not indeed
οὗτος, αὕτη, τοῦτο, *pronoun*, this
ὀφείλω, *v.tr.*, owe
ὀφθαλμός, *n.*, eye
ὄψις, *n.*, faculty of sight
ὄψον, *n.*, food other than bread, cakes, etc. (see 332 d n.)

πάγκαλος, *adj.*, splendid, glorious (*adv.*, -ως)
παγκρατιαστής, *n.*, all-round athlete (338. c, n.)
πάθος, *n.*, emotion ; suffering
παῖς, *n.*, boy, servant
πάλαι, *adv.*, of old : παλαιός, *adj.*, ancient
πάλιν, *adv.*, back, again
παμπόνηρος, *adj.*, wholly wicked
παννυχίς, *n.*, all-night festival
πάππος, *n.*, grandfather
παντάπασι, *adv.*, altogether
πανταχοῦ, *adv.*, everywhere
πάντως, *adv.*, certainly, by all means
πάνυ, *adv.*, precisely : οὐ π., not exactly
πάππος, *n.*, grandfather

παρά, *prep.* (1) *c.gen.*, from : (2) *c.dat.*, at, among : (3) *c.accus.*, towards, on account of
παρά, compounds of—
παραγίγνομαι, *intr.*, be present at
— δίδωμι, *tr.*, pass on
— ειμι, *intr.*, be present
— ἔχω, *tr.*, provide
— ἵημι, *tr.*, admit. **See** 341 b n.
— κάθημαι, *v.intr.*, sit beside
— κατατίθημι, *v.tr.*, deposit
— λαμβάνω, *v.tr.*, accept, take over
— νομῶ, *v.tr.*, act contrary to law
— σκευάζω, *v.tr.*, provide, invent
— φέρω, *v.tr.*, carry along
παραμύθιον, *n.*, consolation
παραπλήσιος, *adj.*, similar
παροιμία, *n.*, proverb
πᾶς, πᾶσα, πᾶν, *adj.*, all ; the whole ; every
πάσχω, *v.tr.* (*aor.* ἔπαθον), suffer ; experience, feel
πατάσσω, *v.tr.*, strike
πατήρ, *n.*, father
παύω, *v.tr.*, check : *middle*, παύομαι, make an end of, cease
παχύνω, *v.tr.*, fatten
πείθω, *v.tr.*, persuade
πειρῶ, *v.intr.*, attempt, try
πέμπω, *v.tr.*, send, escort ; *cf.* πομπή
πενία, *n.*, poverty
πέπονθεν, *from* πέπονθα, *perf. of* πάσχω
περαίνω, *v.tr.*, accomplish
περί, *prep. c.gen.*, about, around ; also with dat. and accus.
περί, compounds of—
περίειμι, *intr.*, go around (*pres. part.*, περιϊών)
— ἵστημι, *tr.* or *intr.*, place around : περιειστήκει, had come round

περίειμι, go around
— μένω, await
— ὁρῶ, v.tr., overlook
περιμαχητός, adj., fought for
πεττός, n., piece (at chess) :
adj., -ευτικός, chess-player
πέφυκα, see φύω
πῇ, interrog., how? (πη, enclitic,
in some way)
πλεῖστος, superl. of πολύς, most
πλεονεκτῶ, v.intr., gain unfair
advantage, claim more than
one's due
πλέω, v.intr., sail, go on a voyage
πλῆθος, n., number, abundance
πλήν, prep. or conj., except,
except if
πλίνθος, n., brick
πλοῖον, n., ship
πλούσιος, adj., wealthy
πλοῦτος, n., wealth (v.intr.,
πλουτῶ)
ποθῶ, v.tr., long for
ποιητής, n., poet
ποιμαίνω, v.tr., tend sheep
ποιμήν, n., shepherd (adj., -ενικός)
ποῖος, interrog. pron., of what kind
ποιῶ, v.tr., make, do : ὑφ'
ἑαυτοὺς ποιεῖσθαι, bring under
their control
πολέμιος, adj., enemy
πολεμῶ, v.intr., carry on war
πόλις, n., city
πολιτεία, n., government, constitution
πολίτης, n., citizen (adj., -ικός,
civil, political)
πολλάκις, adv., many times ; often
πολύς, πολλή, πολύ, adj., much,
many : ὡς τὸ πολύ, for the
most part
πολύστροφος, adj., changing,
versatile (Pindar)
πομπή, n., procession, escort
πονηρός, adj., wicked, rotten ;
(-ία, n., wickedness)
πόρρω, adv., far ; far away from
πόσις, n., drinking

πότε, interrog., when? (ποτε,
enclitic, sometimes)
πότερος, interrog. adj., which? :
πότερον . . . ἤ, whether . . . or?
ποτόν, n., drink, beverage
πότος, n., drinking-party
ποῦ, interrog., where? (που,
enclitic, surely, doubtless)
πρᾶγμα, n., thing, affair : in
plural, trouble
πρᾶξις, n., action
πρᾶος, adj., mild, gentle
πράττω, v.tr., do, achieve : εὖ
or καλῶς πρ., succeed, prosper :
πράττομαι, demand payment
πρέπω, v.intr., be fitting
πρεσβύτης, n., old man
πρίασθαι, v.tr., buy
πρίν, prep. and conj., before
πρό, prep. c.gen., before, in preference to
πρόβατον, n., sheep
προθυμοῦμαι, v.intr., strive, be
keen
προλέγω, v.tr., foretell, warn ;
aor. προεῖπον
προῖκα, adv., gratis, for nothing
προπηλάκισις, n., insulting behaviour
πρός, prep. (1) c.accus., towards :
(2) c.dat., at, in addition to
πρός, compounds of—
προσαγορεύω, tr., address, call
— βλέπω, tr., look at
— γίγνομαι, intr., be added to
— δέομαι, tr., need also
— ἥκω, intr., belong to, be
fit
— εἰμι, intr., be added
— ἔρχομαι, intr., approach
— εὔχομαι (fut. -ευξ-), intr.,
pray
— ποιοῦμαι, intr., pretend
— πολεμῶ, intr., make war
against
— τάττω, tr., command
— τίθημι, tr., add
— χρῶμαι, tr., use in addition

προσῆκον, τό, part. of προσήκω, what is fitting

πρόσθεν, prep. and adv., before

προσθήκη, n., addition

προσκεφάλαιον, n., cushion

πρότερος, adj., prior

προτίθημι, v.tr., propose (whence aorist. mid., προὐθέμεθα)

πρῶτος, adj., first

πυκνά, adv., frequently (compar. -ότερον)

πυκτικός, adj., of boxing

πυνθάνομαι, v.tr., inquire ; (aor.), discover by inquiry

πω, adv., yet : πώποτε, ever yet

πῶς, interrog., how ? πως, enclitic, in some way

ῥᾴδιος, adj., easy : adv., ῥᾳδίως, superl., ῥᾷστα

ῥῆμα, n., saying, expression ; λέγομεν τῷ ῥήματι οὕτως, we express ourselves in this way

ῥήτωρ, n., speaker, counsel

σαρδάνιος, adj., sardonic (see 337 a n.)

σαφής, adj., plain, clear ; adv., -ῶς

σημαίνω, v.tr., mean, indicate

σιτίον, n., food, diet

σκέπτομαι (aor. ἐσκεψάμην), v.tr., inquire

σκέψις, n., inquiry

σκοπῶ, v.tr., look, inquire

σκυτοτομικός, adj., of the shoe-maker

σκώπτω, v.intr. or tr., make fun of, jest

σμικρός, adj., small, slight

σμίλη, n., chisel

σός, adj. of σύ, your (sing.)

σοφία, n., wisdom, skill, cleverness

σοφός, adj., wise, clever

σπουδάζω, v.intr., be serious, strive

σπουδαῖος, adj., serious ; honour-able.

στερεός, adj., hard, solid, firm

στέρομαι, v.tr., deprive

στεφανῶ, v.tr., crown : (passive) wear a garland

στρατόπεδον, n., camp, army

στρέφω, v.tr., turn, twist, torment

σύ, σέ, pron., you (singular)

συκοφάντης, n., slanderer. See 340 d n.

συκοφαντῶ, v.tr. or intr., slander, attack unfairly

συλλήβδην, adv., all together, wholesale

συμφέρον, τό, one's advantage

σύν, prep. c.dat., with

σύν, compounds of—

συναορῶ, intr., accompany

συμβαίνω, intr., happen, result

συμβάλλω, tr., compare : middle, contribute

συγγίγνομαι, intr., meet, have an affair with

σύνειμι, intr., come together

συνίημι, tr., understand

συμμαχῶ, intr., be allied to

σύνοιδα, intr., be aware, be conscious of

συνομολογῶ, tr., allow, agree to

σύμφέρω, intr., be advanta-geous

σύμφημι, tr., consent to

συγχωρῶ, tr., allow, concede

συνειδώς, part. of σύνοιδα

συνῆκα, aor. of συνίημι

σφόδρα, adv., much, exceedingly

σχολή, n., leisure : adv., σχολῇ, scarcely, by no means

σῶμα, n., body

σῶς, adj., safe

σωτηρία, n., safety, preservation

σωφρονῶ, v.intr., be sane, be of sound mind

σώφρων, adj., sane, self-controlled; adv, σωφρόνως

τἀναντία, etc., see ἐναντία, etc.

ταύτῃ, adv., in this way

τελευτῶ, (1) v.tr., complete : (with omission of βίον), die : (2) v.intrans., come to an end ; τελευτῶν, finally

τε, part., and ; both

τέλεος, adj., perfect, complete ; adv., τελέως

τέλος, n., end

τετράκις, four times : τέτταρα, four (neut.)

τέχνη, n., art, craft

τέως, adv., till then

τῆδε, adv., thus

τίθημι, v.tr., place, ordain : middle, establish. See 338 E n.

τιμή, n., honour, reputation

τίμιος, adj., honoured, precious

τίς (interrog.), who, what ? (enclitic), someone, something

τίτθη, n., nurse

τοί, particle, exactly, indeed

τοίνυν, particle, therefore

τοιοῦτος and τοιόσδε, adj., such, cf. οἷος

τοιχωρύχος, n., thief, house-breaker

τολμῶ, v.tr. or intr., dare, venture

τοσόνδε, adj., this much (alluding to what follows)

τοσοῦτος, adj., so great, so much

τότε, adv., then

τραχύς, -εῖα, -ύ, adj., rough, rugged

τρεῖς, τρία, num., three

τρέχω, v.intr., run (aor. ἔδραμον)

τρίς, adv., thrice

τρόπος, n., manner, character

τυγχάνω, v., (1) obtain, τινός : (2) happen

τυραννίς, n., tyranny

τυραννῶ, v.intr., rule tyrannically

τυφλότης, n., blindness

ὑγίεια, n., health

ὑγιής, adj., healthy, sound

ὑγραίνω, v.tr., moisten

ὕθλος, n., chatter, nonsense

ὑμεῖς, pron., you (plural)

ὑμνῶ, v.tr., sing, proclaim ; repeat, recite

ὑπέθου, see ὑποτίθημι

ὑπέρ, prep., (1) c.gen., on behalf of, about : (2) c.accus., beyond

ὕπνος, n., sleep

ὑπό, prep., (1) c.gen., beneath ; by the help of : (2) c.accus., beneath

ὑπό, compounds of—

ὑπάρχω, intr., be available

— ηρετῶ, intr., serve (τινί)

ὑποκατακλίνομαι, intr., yield one's place to, defer to

— λαμβάνω, v.tr. and intr., think, judge ; interrupt

— λογίζομαι, tr., take into account

— μένω, intr., remain : tr., expect

— τίθημι, tr., place beneath ; assume (in argument)

— τρέμω, intr., tremble

ὑπόδημα, n., shoe

ὑπολογιστέον, gerundive of ὑπολογίζομαι

ὑποψία, n., suspicion

ὕστερος, adj., later

φαίνω, v.tr., reveal ; (middle), appear, seem : aor. pass., ἐφάνην

φανερός, adj., obvious (adv., -ῶς)

φάσκω, v.tr., allege

φαῦλος, adj., poor, mean

φέρω, v.tr., carry, bear : φέρε δή, well now . . . : χαλεπῶς φ., endure hardly, be vexed at

φημί, v.tr., say

φθέγγομαι, v.tr., utter, pronounce

φθονῶ, v.tr., envy ; refuse from envy, grudge

φιλάργυρος, adj., money-loving

φιλία, n., love, friendship

φιλονεικῶ, v.intr., strive, insist

φίλος, n., friend

φιλότιμος, adj., ambitious (v.intr., -τιμοῦμαι)

φλυαρῶ, v.tr., talk nonsense (n., φλυαρία)

φοβοῦμαι, v.intr., be afraid

φοιτῶ, v.intr., visit frequently

φρόνιμος, adj., wise

φροντίζω, v.intr., give attention to

φροντίς, n., attention, anxiety

φύλαξ, n., guard

φυλάττω, v.tr., guard ; keep safe ; retain (a position in argument) : (middle), guard against

φύσις, n., nature

φύω, v.tr., produce, generate ; intrans., especially in perf. πέφυκα, be by nature

φώρ, n., thief

χαίρω, v.intr.,. enjoy (τινί), be glad

χαλεπαίνω, v.intr., be angry with (τινί)

χαλεπός, adj., difficult, unpleasant

χαρίεις, adj., graceful, charming, witty (adv., -έντως)

χαρίζομαι, v.tr., grant as a favour

χάρις, n., charm ; gratitude

χείρων, adv., worse

χθές, adv., yesterday

χορδή, n., string, chord

χρεία, n., need, use

χρή, v.impers., one must, one should

χρῆμα, n., thing :   χρήματα, goods, money

χρηματιστής, n., money-maker

χρῆσις, n., use : -σιμος, useful

χρηστός, adj., good, beneficial

χρόνος, n., time :   διὰ χρόνου, after a long interval

χρυσίον, n., gold

χρῶμαι, v.tr., use (τινί)

ψεύδομαι, v.tr. or intr., deceive, lie

ψυχή, n., soul

ψύχω, v.tr., cool

ὡρμημένοι, ὥρμησαν, see ὁρμῶ

ὠνόμασα, see ὀνομάζω

ὧδε, adv., thus

ὡς, conj., (1) as, (2) that, (3) because

ὡσαύτως, adv., in the same way

ὦσι, third pers. pres. subj. of εἰμί

ὥσπερ, adv., as though, as

ὥστε, conj., so that (Latin ita ... ut)

ὦτα, plural of οὖς

ὠφελία, n., profit :   adj., -ιμος, profitable

ὠφελῶ, v.tr., help, benefit